Working in the Gig Economy

Working in the Gig Economy

How to thrive and succeed when you chose to work for yourself

Thomas Oppong

KoganPage

First published in Great Britain and the United States in 2019 by Kogan Page Limited

2nd Floor, 45 Gee Street	c/o Martin P Hill Consulting	4737/23 Ansari Road
London EC1V 3RS	122 W 27th St, 10th Floor	Daryaganj
United Kingdom	New York NY 10001	New Delhi 110002
www.koganpage.com	USA	India

© Thomas Oppong 2019

The right of Thomas Oppong to be identified as the author of this work has been asserted by him in accordance with the Copyright, Designs and Patents Act 1988.

ISBN   978 0 7494 8355 5
E-ISBN   978 0 7494 8356 2

British Library Cataloguing-in-Publication Data

A CIP record for this book is available from the British Library.

Library of Congress Cataloging-in-Publication Data

Names: Oppong, Thomas, author.
Title: Working in the gig economy : how to thrive and succeed when you choose to work for yourself / Thomas Oppong.
Description: London ; New York : Kogan Page, 2019. | Includes bibliographical references and index.
Identifiers: LCCN 2018036793 (print) | LCCN 2018039493 (ebook) | ISBN 9780749483562 (ebook) | ISBN 9780749483555
Subjects: LCSH: Self-employed. | Hours of labor.
Classification: LCC HD8036 (ebook) | LCC HD8036 .O66 2019 (print) | DDC 650.1–dc23
LC record available at https://catalog.loc.gov/vwebv/search?searchCode=LCCN&searchArg=2018036793&searchType=1&permalink=y

Typeset by Integra Software Services, Pondicherry
Print production managed by Jellyfish
Printed and bound by CPI Group (UK) Ltd, Croydon, CR0 4YY

CONTENTS

Supreme Court ruling 2018

On 13 June 2018 the British Supreme Court ruled that Gary Smith, employed by Pimlico Plumbers as a self-employed plumber, was entitled to workers' rights such as sick pay and holiday, following a dispute over his employment status.

Even though there is no guarantee that similar cases will be decided in the same way, the decision has set a strong precedent for anyone working in the gig economy. The ruling is likely to be used by regulators to amend the employment law to protect the self-employed and offer them more protection. Thousands of gig workers are set to benefit in different ways in the future, especially those who work for single employers.

'This is one of the biggest decisions ever made by the courts on workers' rights. Thousands of workers like Gary Smith could now find themselves with the added security of benefits like sick pay and holiday pay,' says Rebecca Hilsenrath, Equality and Human Rights Commission Chief Executive.

The Supreme Court ruling is a step closer to clarifying the issue of the employment status of gig workers.

Introduction

The future is here. The workforce of the future is mobile, adaptable and flexible. Actors, musicians and seasonal farm workers have always migrated from gig to gig for many years, but in recent years the trend has undergone a continuous change and expanded into different industries. Short-term on-demand talent is in high demand.

The gig economy is a fast-growing pool of short-term independent contractors and freelancers. It is becoming a viable alternative to traditional nine-to-five work. A growing body of research points to the continuous growth of flexible workers. McKinsey has predicted that by 2025 over 60 million people around the world could benefit from the growth of talent platforms that help people find freelance work that suits their skills. As the gig economy grows, it will open new opportunities for highly skilled and dynamic individuals who expect more than a stable and secure job.

Millions of people and thousands of companies have already benefited from the new, modern world of work. The gig economy empowers people, both skilled and unskilled, to manage their time, work and how much they earn without committing to traditional long-term contracts. The growth of the gig economy has been largely influenced by technology, and the changing work culture across the world. As the pace of technology increases, millions of people are finding new ways to boost their income. The new reality is that you can leverage technology to get paid for your work. People who have mastered their craft don't need permission to profit from their skills. They no longer have to wait to be chosen. With the right tools, you can work from anywhere, on any device, and collaborate with people you've never met. Technology is empowering people to earn money on their own terms, but the growth of the gig economy is not limited to digital technologies. Contractors, freelancers and part-time workers from all industries are choosing to work for themselves. Work processes are changing to support the agile, flexible and mobile workforce.

The transformative growth of the gig economy is leading to an increased specialization of skill. Building a career as an expert is increasingly becoming the ultimate form of career insurance. Today, it's easier to earn income from multiple sources as an expert. There is no cap on what you can earn, other than your available productive time. The promise of freedom, flexibility, control and a bigger, better and more creative career makes independent work an attractive option for millions of people across the world.

This book aims to provide practical ideas to help you leverage the gig economy, validate your ideas for independent work, launch a purposeful career and build a successful personal brand, and succeed as a gig worker when you embrace the gig economy. It's a guide for embracing the freelance lifestyle, with practical examples and rich experiences of people who have succeeded in the gig economy. It will prepare you to face the future with confidence.

My favourite part of writing this book has been interviewing interesting people who tell their stories about why they've embrace independent work, and how it's benefited both their profits and happiness. *Working in the Gig Economy* is your guide to building the life you want and thriving in the gig economy. The gig economy is poised for growth, and *Working in the Gig Economy* will prepare you to build a career that can stand the test of time and enable you to live your life on your own terms.

01
The emergence and evolution of the gig economy

This chapter will provide an overview of the gig economy. We will examine the gig economy in detail and how it works. We begin with the meaning of 'gig economy' and discuss the importance of flexible work and the many opportunities it offers to gig workers. We will explain the different categories of independent work, the major difference between gig work and zero-hour contracts, how gig contractors find work, how you can leverage, and the many opportunities the gig economy offers you to build your ideal future. We will clarify the difference between gig workers, consultants, independent contractors and freelancers. We will also discuss the impact of on-demand platforms on the gig economy, why the gig economy trend keeps rising and the future of workforce management. We complete the chapter with employment rights for gig workers.

What is the gig economy?

The gig economy is a term that captures the idea of short-term work that offers flexibility with regard to work hours. The phrase 'gig economy' was coined at the height of the financial crisis early in 2009, when people who were unemployed made a living by gigging, or working, several part-time jobs wherever they could (Hook, 2015). In a speech given at Bradford's National Science and Media Museum on 20 June 2017, Andrew G. Haldane, Chief Economist of the Bank of England, said, 'Prior to the Industrial Revolution, and indeed for some years after it, most workers were self-employed or worked in small businesses. There were no unions. Hours were flexible, depending on what work was needed to collect the crops, milk the cows or put bread on the table' (Bank of England, 2017). While it might seem that long-established ways of working are being disrupted, Haldane argues that the one person, one career model existed decades ago. The concept of gig work is not new.

Prior to industrialization in the 19th century, people worked multiple jobs to piece together a living. Flexible and task-based work existed in the past, but it has evolved. Today, people have more options, better platforms and different technologies to advertise and access short-term work.

According to the Cambridge Dictionary, 'a gig economy is a way of working that is based on people having temporary jobs or doing separate pieces of work, each paid separately, rather than working for an employer'. Gig work is normally temporary and often influenced by technology but is not limited to it. Gig workers are referred to as independent contractors, freelancers or self-employed workers. Independent work has a high degree of autonomy, payment is made based on completed tasks, assignments or sales, and workers have short-term relationships with their clients.

Trends in the labour market and the recession have contributed to the growth of the gig economy. It's a growing modern way of work that gives freelancers the independence to manage their work and offers businesses the opportunity to hire from an on-demand global workforce, cutting the cost of recruiting new talent. This new business paradigm empowers individuals to better shape their own destiny and leverage their existing assets to their benefit (McAffee, 2016). There is no one future-proof career, only better options for people who are willing to take control of their future. Work as we know it will continue to change. A new breed of workers is emerging. Change is happening, and accelerating fast. The free exchange of information over data networks is becoming the centre of economic activity. The potential for digital platforms to increase global productivity and shift the world of work is enormous. A thriving marketplace is evolving fast. This has created an on-demand workforce for an on-demand world. Millions of people each year are choosing independent work, freelancing and casual work over job security. It's increasingly popular with both businesses and workers. Uber has over 40,000 drivers in London alone (Uber, 2017). There are five million people (15.6 per cent of the total full-time and part-time workforce of 32 million people) currently working in the gig economy in the UK, according to McKinsey Global Institute (2016). The rapid growth of on-demand workers suggests that this is the future of work. In a PwC survey of over ten thousand members of the general population based in China, Germany, India, the UK and the US, 60 per cent think 'few people will have stable, long-term employment in the future' (PwC, 2017). A growing number of new businesses that can't afford to hire full-time employees rely on gig workers for business administrative support. Digital platforms are connecting independent workers with employers at an increasing rate.

According to McKinsey, 'By 2025 they could add $2.7 trillion to the global GDP and begin to ameliorate many of the persistent problems in the world's labour markets' (McKinsey Global Institute, 2015). Online talent platforms have amplified the many benefits of flexible work through their larger scale, quick matches and simple coordination of work among gig workers and their clients. This improves trust and helps gig workers build rich portfolios that lay strong foundation for more work in the future. The workforce today is increasingly mobile and many jobs can be done and delivered from anywhere. In recent times, work and location have been decoupled.

Gig work is not just limited to Uber, Lyft, Deliveroo, TaskRabbit or UpWork. Not all independent work roles are based around a technology platform. Contract workers can work for traditional companies without using online applications. In fact, technology giants like Amazon have embraced flexible workers. The online retailer is operating a programme called Amazon Flex. The programme works like other on-demand companies, including Uber and Lyft: with an app, a network of short-term contractors can sign up for flexible delivery shifts at a time suitable for them. On the programme's website, Amazon says, 'Amazon Flex provides a flexible opportunity for Delivery Partners looking to turn free time into supplementary income. The available delivery blocks may fluctuate week to week and are not guaranteed' (Deliver smiles). The company allows contract workers to build their own schedule and manage their time.

In a gig economy, contractors are paid per delivery, with no standing wage. They manage their work, finances, reputation and pension. Intuit has predicted that over 40 per cent of the workforce in the US alone will work for themselves. 'We think this has been trending the last few decades,' Alex Chriss, Vice President and General Manager of Self-Employed Solutions at Intuit, said in an interview. Six per cent of the workforce in 1989 had contingent positions, he said. 'We believe it could be 40 per cent of the workforce by 2020' (Pofeldt, 2015).

How the gig economy works

Independent work or short-term contract differs from full-time employment in one important way: the term relates to many one-off tasks or assignments that need to be completed in a specified period of time. Workers are paid based on deliverables, projects completed or work done. In some cases, projects can be ongoing for months or even years, but contractors do not enjoy the benefits of full-time employment. A gig (a single task, assignment or job) usually represents one source of income in a given month or period. When you become a gig worker, you focus on finding, signing and delivering gigs. Some freelancers have multiple gigs they are working on to increase their income. They assemble various income streams and work on those gigs at the same time. Others have full-time jobs but undertake part-time gig work to supplement their income.

For some contractors, when they aggregate a variety of sources of gigs for various clients, their earnings can be less than, or similar to, any full-time workers in their industries. Some short-term contractors can also accumulate higher earnings compared to full-time workers. Gigs are not guaranteed, but it pays to find your niche. People with a variety of skills at all levels can readily and easily secure short-term work faster than skilled workers who rely on just one skill. In the gig economy, independent contractors are responsible for paying their taxes and savings. Self-employment can be extremely rewarding in the long term when you have a consistent stream of income from multiple sources, but it does come with some financial and mental risks.

The importance of flexibility in the gig economy

Globalization has played a key role in the growth of gig workers across the world. Workers in many major developed economies are more agile than ever before. The gig economy offers every independent worker enormous opportunity to choose how they work. A basic element of the gig economy is its flexibility. The idea of working whenever you want, sometimes from wherever you want, depending on the type of work, makes it convenient for millions of people to benefit from their skills without compromising on family, or other priorities.

An increasing number of the working population across the world are choosing self-employment, freelancing and short-term work over job security. Almost three in ten workers worldwide have chosen to work for themselves. Twenty-nine per cent of the global workforce reported being self-employed in 2013, according to Gallup, a research-based consultancy company (Ryan, 2014). In a FlexJobs 2017 Work Flex Super Survey of more than 5,500 people, 62 per cent of respondents said they've left or have considered leaving a job because it did not offer flexible work options (Reynolds, 2017). People are choosing flexibility over stability. Flexibility is becoming more important than ever, even to full-time workers. Independent workers often enjoy higher job satisfaction as they have the choice as to when, where and how they work. The global reality is that many employers are losing the control they once had over the labour market. According to a PwC report, the 'desire for autonomy is strongest in China, especially among young people, indicating a generational shift towards greater freedom, entrepreneurship, and specialist skills in this rapidly evolving economy' (PwC, 2017).

The 'Workforce marketplace: Invent your own future' report argues that in the next five years everything we assume about 'full time employment and freelancers will flip completely' (Accenture, 2017). In Chapter 10 we will discuss a few of the many platforms that help freelancers to find relevant work. Businesses advertise short-term jobs and gig workers apply for relevant gigs that match their skills.

The gig economy offers people the rare opportunity to do important work at a convenient time when they are more productive. The prospect of a stable income has changed. Employers don't guarantee job security anymore. Employees are dispensable until they prove their value to their employer. In many cases, they are overworked and underpaid. Many employees are not content with their full-time jobs.

According to the London School of Business and Finance, which interviewed 1,000 professionals of different age groups from across the UK, an overwhelming 47 per cent want to change jobs, and more than one in five are looking to career hop in the next 12 months (Burn-Callander, 2015). Eighty-five per cent of workers worldwide admit to hating their jobs when surveyed anonymously, according to a Gallup poll (Clifton, 2017). The gig economy offers enormous options for people of all skill sets. Not only does the rising change in work trends make it possible for people to pursue self-employment, it's also the way more people seem to actually want to work. The opportunities the gig economy offers mean that people are no longer bound to the traditional career paths. The modern worker wants more control of their work-life.

The growth of independent work

A McKinsey Global Institute report suggests that the phenomenon of independent work is more widespread than official data suggest. According to the study, between 20 and 30 per cent of people in the US and Europe are independent workers. 'Our survey finds that the majority of independent workers in all countries participate by choice,' said Susan Lund, a partner at the McKinsey Global Institute. She said it was 'especially well-suited to seniors, stay-at-home caregivers, and young people – all large and growing demographic groups with an interest in working but with significant time commitments or reluctance to take 9-to-5 jobs' (O'Connor, 2016). Millions of people are choosing to pursue independent work for freedom and flexibility. People are willing to put in more effort and time if they can do the work on their own terms. Samsung predicts that, by 2020, 40 per cent of the global workforce will be self-employed (Samsung at Work, 2017).

The proliferation of online platforms has made access to work easier than ever before. People have more control over when, where and how much they work. According to Indeed, an online recruitment platform, 'Interest in flexible work increased by 42.1 per cent from 2013 to 2015 in nine of the 12 largest economies in the world' (Indeed, 2016).

One in three Americans is an independent worker, according to a report commissioned by Freelancer's Union and Elance-oDesk (MarketWired, 2014). And 34 per cent of America's workforce qualify as independent workers, according to the same report conducted by the independent research firm Edelman Berland. As businesses continue to embrace on-demand talent and focus on improving efficiency and cutting costs, this number can only increase. In the UK, 15 per cent of the total workforce is self-employed, according to a report by the Office for National Statistics (ONS). The report also states that self-employment is at its highest level since records began about forty years ago. The ONS says, 'The self-employment share of all employment has risen more quickly than its share of total hours worked, highlighting the importance of part-time self-employment in supporting recent trends' (Office for National Statistics, 2016).

Categories of independent work

Despite many similarities in how they work, there a number of different categories of gig workers that encompass a wide range of behaviours and skills. In practice, there are two major groups of gig workers in the gig economy. The first is made up of independent contractors who get most of their work from online platforms. The second group consists of less skilled gig workers providing transportation services and 'concierge services', such as household tasks and delivery of goods and services. In recent times, the media and policy makers have criticized how employers treat their workforce in this category. However, the different types of gig workers extend beyond skilled and unskilled workers.

People who make passive income by renting rooms on Airbnb are completely different from skilled workers who are fully committed to working to make a living. Every short-term worker falls into one of four categories of gig workers. According to McKinsey Global Institute, and as visualized in the following box, the groups of contingent workers are: free agents, casual earners, reluctant gig workers and financially strapped contract workers (McKinsey Global Institute, 2016).

Different types of independent workers

- **Free agents** – Active freelancers who choose to work in the gig economy even though they can work as full-time employers. They prefer to be self-employed.

- **Casual earners** – These workers have full-time jobs, but they choose to do gig work to bring in extra cash or fulfil a creative ambition.

- **Reluctant gig workers** – These workers choose the gig economy because they can't find traditional jobs. They are prepared to give up gig work for full-time jobs.

- **Financially strapped contract workers** – These workers choose gig work out of necessity rather than choice because their primary source of income is not sufficient.

While full-time independent work may be generally appealing to millions of people, it's not for everyone. People are working in different capacities, even as independent workers. As widely available as short-term work is, the workers who pursue it have different reasons for choosing self-employment. Free agents are fully committed to gig work, even despite the opportunities traditional work offers. Reluctant gig workers and financially strapped contract workers don't see gig work as their primary source of income and are prepared to give up short-term work when they find favourable conditions in full-time work. Free agents and casual workers are more likely to find fulfilment in what they do than those who do gig work out of necessity (reluctant and financially strapped contract workers). According to the McKinsey survey, 'Free agents reported higher levels of satisfaction in multiple dimensions of their work lives than those holding traditional jobs by choice.'

Gig workers, consultants, independent contractors, and freelancers – what is the difference?

People use different terms when discussing self-employment. These terms can sometimes be confusing when used interchangeably.

- **Gig workers** – Gig is a term borrowed from the music industry, where musicians move to different venues to perform for an audience for defined time. A gig is 'a single performance by a musician or group of musicians, especially playing modern or pop music' (Cambridge Dictionary). Today, 'gig workers' refer to temporary workers in many industries who primarily focus on short-term work for a fee. They get paid for 'gigs' they deliver to clients.

- **Consultants** – Generally, consultants advise or consult for a fee based on time spent or for a given period. They work in almost every industry you can think of. Consultants mainly provide professional advice to their clients for a fixed fee. On-demand consultants in the gig economy work in the same scope. Gig workers can work as consultants and any business can also register to provide consultancy services. Large corporations like McKinsey & Co, PwC and Deloitte Consulting provide various consulting services to major brands in the world.

- **Independent contractors** – Independent contractors are highly skilled self-employed workers who provide temporary or supplemental work on a project-to-project basis. Contracts normally include start and end dates. A contractor can be a single person or business that provides goods or services to clients based on an agreed contract. They are usually paid on completion of a project or work for a period of time.

- **Freelancers** – A freelancer is a flexible self-employed worker who provides short-term services to multiple clients at the same time for a fixed rate. Freelancers are free to work from anywhere, away from their client's offices, but they communicate with their clients regularly to update them about the progress of their work. They manage their own schedule and negotiate their own terms. Some freelancers are employees who work part-time to supplement their income. Freelancers are popular in the creative industry.

The difference between gig work and zero-hour contracts

The most important similarity between zero-hour contracts and working as an independent contractor is that in both cases people work on demand, as and when work is available. And the flexibility gig workers enjoy is also available to zero-hour contractors. Zero-hour contracts are specific agreements employers use that does not guarantee consistent work.

There is no guaranteed work, hours, sick pay, pensions, redundancy entitlements or notice periods. Workers agree to work as and when needed. Zero-hours contractors (also referred to as casual workers) are globally used by retailers, restaurants, hotels and the leisure industry. Zero-hour contracts are usually for 'piece work' or 'on call' work, e.g. interpreters,' they are on call to work when you need them. Employees who work as zero-hour contractors are free to accept or refuse the work.

In the UK, 'zero-hour workers are entitled to statutory annual leave and the national minimum wage in the same way as full-time workers' (Gov.uk).

Gig workers have no 'employee status' and they choose to work on projects that matches their skill set. Whilst gig workers are paid based on tasks performed or delivered, zero-hour contractors are paid per hour. But people on zero-hour contracts can also supplement their incomes with work in the gig economy. One important similarity between zero-hour contractors and gig consultants is that both categories of workers enjoy the flexibly of work – they make arrangements about working conditions that suit them and schedule their working hours.

How gig workers find on-demand work

As the gig economy proliferates, independent professionals are increasingly becoming an integral part of the modern workforce. As the flexible work lifestyle grows in popularity, the number of contract work resources has increased to match the demand.

To succeed as a gig worker, you have to establish a great portfolio (a combination of your best past work – it's the compelling reason you give to persuade clients to hire you). And you can only build an amazing profile if you consistently work and complete jobs. Finding the right short-term work can be challenging if you don't know where to look and who to contact. Many contingent workers give up easily because they have no clue how to actually find clients. But if you start with good research and ask the right businesses, you will begin to grow a network of prospective clients who can offer you work consistently to sustain your chosen career option.

Here is a good approach for starting out as an independent worker:

1 Build an online portfolio that outlines your expertise, work experience, what you have been able to achieve and clients you have worked with in the past.

2 Start educating your audience for free through blogging about your industry.

3 Research and find out prospective clients who have worked with independent contractors in the past. You can easily put together a list by checking out client lists of successful freelancers in your industry.

4 Reach out to the clients to learn more about why they work with particular groups of on-demand workers, the problems contract workers solve for them and how they found them. You won't get a response from every one of them but a few may reply to give you an idea of what clients expect from on-demand workers and how best to position yourself in your industry. The best way to improve your chances of getting a reply is to be concise, brief and specific, and to make your questions simple and easy to answer (no more than three questions).

Example:

Subject: [Name], I'd like to know more about your business.

Hello [Name],

Your business solves a unique problem in the industry. You solve the problem of _____really well.

I'm a [state what you do], and I was wondering if you could spare some time to help answer a few questions about your business and how you engage the services of short-term consultants. I under-stand you're busy. This will take less than five minutes.

What qualities do you look for when you select on-demand workers?

What problems do gig workers generally solve for your business?

Thank you for your time!

Looking forward to helping your business grow.

Best regards,

[Your name]

---

5 Don't ask for work. Ask for advice. Let them know you want to learn. It pays to understand what your potential clients want first before pitching for work. Make a list of companies you want to work for.

6 When you start pitching prospective clients, offer to take on an existing problem. For example, if their business site or blog could do better, offer ideas that can help them stand out, improve their existing solution or help them get more clients. Show them specific ideas to make their business better. Don't come across as desperate. Clients need to see you as in-demand, in control and professional.

7 Don't just rely on cold emails. Use job boards. Platforms like Upwork, PeoplePerHour, Freelancer, WeWorkRemotely and a dozen others spring up every year. And when you register, apply for many relevant jobs, become a fire-horse of pitches. Lead with solutions, not problems. If you are starting out, bid on as many projects as you can.

8 If you are not selected for a project, ask the company if you can stay in touch. They may have future work that fits your profile or skill.

9 Join on-demand groups and meet-ups, attend events and talk to independent workers in your field at popular co-working spaces in your city. Again, approach them as a learner, ask for their advice on finding work and soon you will build your own list of clients who can offer you jobs as and when they become available.

10 And finally, in all circumstances, do your research and approach prospective clients with solutions. This cannot be stressed enough. Be persistent. Don't give up because it's not working for you. Tenacity pays off in the end.

If you pursue an independent work career path, give yourself time to find clients. Be patient and gather advice and feedback along the way whilst doing more of what works.

The impact of technology in the gig economy

Technology is redefining how most things work, from the way we communicate to the way we do business. It facilitates an easy and smooth interaction between people, machines and software across the world. Many online platforms were launched in the past ten years. Pioneers like Uber, Fiverr, Lyft and IKEA's recently acquired TaskRabbit continue to attract venture capital, users and customers. These platforms strategically match short-term workers with clients who are willing to pay for services delivered on a short-term basis. They provide services from simple online tasks like providing feedback to complex tasks like providing medical advice.

Didi-Chuxing, China's biggest Uber alternative, has registered over 15 million licensed drivers. 'With the rise of the service industry and online platforms, people can directly translate their time and skills into production power, and digital payment tools make it possible for them to get paid wherever and whenever they work,' said Hao Jian, chief consultant at China's largest online recruiting firm Zhaopin.com in Beijing. 'No need to work in cubicles, no need to work for the same old boss' (Jing, 2017). Technology continues to make it easy for skilled workers anywhere in the world to find relevant work.

While technology is critically perceived as a threat to full-time work, it's also the future of work, as long as we make ourselves continually relevant to the fast-changing work environment. The rise of digital platforms is increasingly making it easy for people in any geographical location to benefit from the gig economy. Opportunities for work are open to all qualified workers. The digital age has disrupted the workforce model. Consumer expectations continue to change with time. Customers expect quick delivery of products and services. To keep up with customer demands, businesses are forced to innovate on-demand.

Leveraging independent work marketplaces

Online work marketplaces are connecting on-demand workers and clients like never before, matching skills to employer, capital to investor and consumer to supplier. On sites like PeoplePerHour, UpWork and Freelancer, both employers and contract workers are connecting from all parts of the world to get work done. Some marketplaces are geared for specific industries and niches, whilst others can be used for general tasks like writing, design, software development, engineering, sales, marketing, legal, accounting, business administration and consulting. For employers, it's a lot of on-demand talent in one place for all their short-term projects. And gig workers get all the exposure they need to secure multiple jobs.

On many online marketplaces, clients simply post projects with a detailed description and estimated budget to attract the right expert. Freelancers secure jobs by bidding for them. Prospective clients review bids from gig workers and choose suitable candidates they want to work with. In many cases, the client can begin a conversation with the contractor for further negotiation and in-depth project discussions. Many contingent workers also write proposals to convince clients to choose them over others. Clients review proposals based on a number of factors, including portfolios, profiles, ratings or testimonials. Upon reaching the final agreements, the client will select a qualified contractor and proceed to payment, which is normally held in escrow (a financial arrangement where the payment is held by a third-party app on behalf of transacting parties, pending project completion and approval by the client). Once the final result is delivered by the freelancer, the client will review, request necessary adjustments if any, and give reviews and ratings for the independent worker.

Most projects on freelance marketplaces are bigger in scope, requirements are complex, more valuable, and can take longer than planned to finish, hence requiring more thorough consideration. The best contract workers are often in high demand and have many ongoing projects with a long list of new projects to come. Popular freelancers who consistently deliver amazing results are normally invited to bid on projects from the same client in the future. This makes it easy for clients to work with the same professional in their field without wasting time reviewing profiles or browsing through an entire marketplace for a suitable match. To improve your chances of getting more jobs on short-term work marketplaces, it's important to build your profile right. Ask happy clients to share positive reviews.

A great way to gain experience

When you choose to work full-time, you are committing yourself to a long-term contract that makes it difficult to gain experience in other fields. If you are open and curious to explore different things, pursuing meaningful or passionate work that brings out the best in you, choose to work for yourself. You can try a gig, explore new industries you find intriguing without making a long-term commitment. This is one of the best ways to find work in a career you will love. While many people seek the flexibility and the opportunity to earn extra income, other independent workers value the experience they gain from short-term project-based work. As companies continue to embrace on-demand talent, the gig economy offers enormous opportunities for even part-time workers who want to supplement their income. You can even find day tasks with small and medium-size businesses and high-tech startups seeking to meet their short-term labour needs. It's a valuable stepping-stone for anyone who is ready to explore a new career. You can use freelancer marketplaces to find multiple income opportunities as a way to augment your existing work arrangements and income. The gig economy is flexible enough for anyone to try it out and find work that best suits their unique skills.

Why the gig economy trend keeps rising

People are considering flexible work for various reasons:

- Full-time jobs no longer guarantee financial security.
- Flexibility continues to be an important factor for workers.

- People are looking for ways to work on their own terms and control their schedules.

- Labour specialization is making it easy for employers to seek services from skilled workers outside the company.

- Companies are becoming more comfortable engaging with freelancers.

- Costs for businesses to hire, train and retain employees continue to rise.

- Companies are seeking ways to be agile and flexible in the future.

- The infrastructure that supports independent work continues to grow.

A new direction for talent management

Businesses, and even self-employed individuals, need to be prepared for a possible, even seemingly unlikely, future of work. Planning for the skills needed now and in the future is hard. To keep up with change, business leaders are constantly exploring new roles and skills that can help their businesses run smoothly and take advantage of emerging technology at the same time. And most importantly where they can find the top talent they need. One of the best ways to meet the changing expectations of customers is to access highly skilled professionals for innovative projects that can help businesses stand the test of time. In most cases, the most qualified people for many innovative projects are found outside the company. Many of them work as contractors.

Creative business professionals who offer the right ideas to help businesses succeed often work on innovative problems on a contract basis.

Technology has created a flexible way to do tasks faster, and sometimes even better. As businesses seek to rigorously manage costs and improve efficiency, they often look to flexible options to increase productivity. In a gig economy, businesses save costs in terms of office space and benefits for full-time employees. Many businesses are adapting to the new paradigm of getting work done.

A blended workforce of full-time, part-time, contractor and on-demand talent is on the rise. In as much as employers benefit from an independent workforce, challenges like loyalty, confidentiality, competition and corporate culture need to be constantly addressed to make the process of work easier and better for both parties. The gig economy is expanding participation for both skilled and unskilled labour, providing opportunities for everyone who is ready and willing to work and boosting productivity in an economy. Companies that make talent and capabilities management a matter of urgency are harnessing technological breakthroughs and innovation in their sectors. Top talent is a competitive edge. Successful businesses are building and nurturing adaptability in their workforce by embracing the remote, flexible, on-demand and mobile workforce to enhance productivity and improve customer experience.

Employment rights for gig workers

The world of work has been changing since the Industrial Revolution. Gig workers are not the only ones making the most of their passion and enjoying the flexibility independent work brings. Businesses are also leveraging the opportunities the gig economy presents to cut costs. Critics of the gig economy have argued that gig work, delivered or performed even under the best of circumstances, is something to be examined and monitored to prevent employers from stripping employees of their basic rights as casual workers.

Many have consistently insisted that gig workers are mostly overworked and underpaid, and that employers are offloading risk to 'independent' workers. Others are of the opinion that many contingent workers are subject to exploitation. Many companies that rely on gig workers, contractors and self-employed workers have been involved in public disputes with workers over their work, and whether or not their employees should be classified as gig workers. In 2016 an employment tribunal in the UK ruled Uber drivers were employees, calling the company's self-employment argument 'fictions' and 'twisted language' (Osborne, 2016).

Governments in many countries are not totally blind to the effects the gig economy is having on the rights of independent workers. As a new labour trend, it needs to be regulated but not controlled. The European Union and the UK Government are taking initiatives to understand how the gig economy works. In a report, the Parliamentary Work and Pensions Committee in the UK called for the laws to be changed to prevent gig workers from being exploited by employers. The committee's report found self-employment 'genuinely flexible and rewarding for many'.

> The self-employed are a large and growing part of the UK labour force. Five million people – 15 per cent of workers – are now self-employed, and the expansion of self-employment has played a significant part in current record employment levels. New technology has facilitated the growth of the 'gig economy', which has led to a large number of positive developments and opportunities, as well as continuing to alter the nature of work in many sectors.
>
> (Parliamentary Business, 2017)

The changing face of work will continue to attract the attention of government regulatory bodies in various countries that want to protect citizens' rights and work benefits.

In an independent review of modern working practices commissioned by the British Prime Minister Theresa May on 1 October 2016, Matthew Taylor, Chief Executive of the Royal Society of Arts, called for major changes to law and rules for companies who employ self-employed workers: 'One-sided flexibility is where employers seek to transfer all risk onto the shoulder of workers in ways that make people more insecure and make their lives harder to manage. It's the people told to be ready for work or travelling to work, only to be told none is available', the report stated (Taylor, 2017). In a statement on 11 July 2016 Theresa May said in response to the publication of the review, 'I am clear that this Government will act to ensure that the interests of employees on traditional contracts, the self-employed and those people working in the "gig" economy are all properly protected' (Tara, 2017). The European Union is also seeking more protection and security for citizens who choose to work for themselves, including those on very short-term, part-time and zero-hour contracts. The EU Social Affairs Commissioner Marianne Thyssen said in a news conference, 'We need rules adapted to new forms of work, with adequate protection' (Guarascio, 2017).

The actions of world leaders today will ultimately determine whether both employers and contract workers can maximize the amazing opportunities of the gig economy. The future growth of platform-enabled work depends on initiatives geared towards the improvement of benefits for both businesses and on-demand workers. The gig economy is a rare opportunity to improve work–life balance – we owe it to ourselves to make sure flexible work benefits those who choose self-employment. It's a huge opportunity, not a threat to traditional full-time work. Around the world, many

---

Key takeaways

- The gig economy is a term that captures the idea of short-term work that offers flexibility with regard to work hours.

- Gig work is not just limited to Uber, Lyft, Deliveroo, TaskRabbit or UpWork. Not all independent work roles are based around a technology platform.

- Self-employment can be extremely rewarding in the long term when you have a consistent stream of income from multiple sources, but it does come with financial and mental risks.

- A basic element of the gig economy is its flexibility. The idea of working whenever you want, sometimes from wherever you want, depending on the type of work, makes it convenient for millions of people to benefit from their skills without compromising on family or other priorities.

- Technology is redefining how most things work, from the way we communicate to the way we do business. It facilitates an easy and smooth interaction between people, machines and software across the world.

- As the gig economy proliferates, independent professionals are increasingly becoming an integral part of the modern workforce. As the flexible work lifestyle grow in popularity, the number of contract work resources out there has also increased.

policymakers are still figuring out and clarifying how project-based workers should be treated under the law. Once the details of policies and employment rights are in place in various countries, it could become more viable for millions of people to choose an independent career.

References

Accenture (2017) Workforce marketplace: Invent your own future [Online] www.accenture.com/us-en/insight-future-workforce-trends

Bank of England (2017) Speech: Work, wages and monetary policy, 201/6 [Online] www.bankofengland.co.uk/publications/Documents/speeches/2017/speech984.pdf

Burn-Callander, R (2015) It's official: Most people are miserable at work, 18/9 [Online] www.telegraph.co.uk/finance/jobs/11871751/Its-official-most-people-are-miserable-at-work.html

Clifton, J (2017) The world's broken workplace, 15/06 [Online] news.gallup.com/opinion/chairman/212045/world-broken-workplace.aspx

Contract types and employer responsibilities [Online] www.gov.uk/contract-types-and-employer-responsibilities/zero-hour-contracts

Deliver smiles [Online] flex.amazon.co.uk

Gov.UK, Contract types and employer responsibilities [Online] www.gov.uk/contract-types-and-employer-responsibilities/zero-hour-contracts

Guarascio, F (2017) EU seeks more protection for Uber-style jobs, 4/8 [Online] uk.reuters.com/article/us-eu-workers-gigeconomy/eu-seeks-more-protection-for-uber-style-jobs-idUKKCN1BZ0OU

Hook, L (2015) Year in a word: Gig economy. *Financial Times*, 29/12 [Online] www.ft.com/content/b5a2b122-a41b-11e5-8218-6b8ff73aae15

Indeed (2016) 16 trends shaping the global economy (and how you hire), 14/6 [Online] blog.indeed.com/2016/06/22/global-economy-employment-trends

Jing, M (2017) Pots of gold await in China's gig economy: How mobile technology is transforming the world's biggest jobs market, 26/2 [Online] www.scmp.com/tech/china-tech/article/2073048/pots-gold-chinas-gig-economy

MarketWired (2014) 53 million Americans now freelance, new study finds, 4/9 [Online] www.marketwired.com/press-release/53-million-americans-now-freelance-new-study-finds-1944057.htm

McAffee, John (2016) The war on the gig economy has turned AirBnb and Uber into a legislative bloodbath, *International Business Times*, 27/4 [Online]: http://www.ibtimes.co.uk/john-mcafee-war-gig-economy-has-turned-airbnb-uber-into-legislative-bloodbath-1557107

McKinsey Global Institute (2015) Connecting talent with opportunity in the digital age, June [Online] www.mckinsey.com/global-themes/employment-and-growth/connecting-talent-with-opportunity-in-the-digital-age

McKinsey Global Institute (2016) Independent work: Choice, necessity, and the gig economy, October [Online] www.mckinsey.com/global-themes/employment-and-growth/independent-work-choice-necessity-and-the-gig-economy

O'Connor, Sarah (2016) World's 'gig economy' larger than thought, 10/10 [Online] www.ft.com/content/c5e07542-8e21-11e6-a72e-b428cb934b78?mhq5j=e6

Office for National Statistics (2016) Trends in self-employment in the UK: 2001 to 2015, 13/7 [Online] www.ons.gov.uk/employmentandlabourmarket/peopleinwork/employmentandemployeetypes/articles/trendsinselfemploymentintheuk/2001to2015

Osborne, H (2016) Uber loses right to classify UK drivers as self-employed 28/10 [Online] www.theguardian.com/technology/2016/oct/28/uber-uk-tribunal-self-employed-status

Parliamentary Business (2017) Self-employment and the gig economy, 29/4 [Online] publications.parliament.uk/pa/cm201617/cmselect/cmworpen/847/84702.htm

Pofeldt, E (2015) Intuit: On-demand workers will more than double by 2020, 13/8 [Online] www.forbes.com/sites/elainepofeldt/2015/08/13/intuit-on-demand-workers-will-more-than-double-by-2020/#44f7aff5c460

PwC (2017) Workforce of the future: The competing forces shaping 2030 [Online] www.pwc.com/gx/en/services/people-organisation/workforce-of-the-future/workforce-of-the-future-the-competing-forces-shaping-2030-pwc.pdf

Reynolds, BW (2017) 2017 annual survey finds workers are more productive at home, and more, 21/8 [Online] www.flexjobs.com/blog/post/productive-working-remotely-top-companies-hiring

Ruth, A (2017) The evolution of the gig economy: Cupcakes to claims inspections, 17/05 [Online] www.entrepreneur.com/article/294159

Ryan, B (2014) Nearly three in 10 workers worldwide are self-employed, 22/8 [Online] news.gallup.com/poll/175292/nearly-three-workers-worldwide-self-employed.aspx

Samsung at Work (2017) Open economy, 2/17 [Online] samsungatwork.com/files/Samsung_OpenEconomy_Report.pdf

Tara, E (2017) Know your rights: What does Matthew Taylor's gig economy review mean if you're self-employed or on a zero-hour contract? 12/7 [Online] www.thesun.co.uk/money/3992952/what-does-the-matthew-taylors-gig-economy-review-mean-if-youre-self-employed-or-on-a-zero-hour-contract

Taylor, M (2017) Good work: The Taylor review of modern working practices, 11/7 [Online] www.gov.uk/government/publications/good-work-the-taylor-review-of-modern-working-practices

Uber (2017) TfL's decision and what it means for you, 27/9 [Online] www.uber.com/en-GB/blog/london/tfls-decision-and-what-it-means-for-you

Wikipedia, Gig (music) 4/10 [Online] en.wikipedia.org/wiki/Gig_(music)

02

Jobs of the future and the portfolio career

When you plan for tomorrow, assume that the work environment will be different. Demand in certain sectors will be higher, whilst demand in others will significantly fall because of automation or outsourcing. Before you build a career in any field, it's important to know what trends are shaping the world of work. As the gig economy expands, independent consultants will work with a growing number of businesses that continue to hire on-demand workers. In this chapter, we will look at the major trends that are shaping the modern workforce, and what you can do to prepare yourself for the world of work. We will also cover the most important skills you need to thrive in the new world of work.

Global trends that will affect your future

Compared to the industrial age, work is no longer predictable, career paths are becoming fluid, and people are embracing the new world of work where flexibility is now more important than ever. In fact, we are on the verge of a massive change in how the economy works and what people do to make a living, and generally how society is organized. Disruption and progress are inevitable, but you can change with the times to stay relevant as the world of work changes. To stay relevant, you have to acquire both hard and soft indispensable skills. You can teach yourself valuable soft skills (personal attributes, personality traits, social and communication abilities) in addition to your expertise (job-specific skill and knowledge you need to perform a task). You can easily adapt to the changing face of work.

Automation

While manufacturing work keeps shrinking due to the ever-growing automation, the on-demand workforce keeps growing at an amazing rate. A Deloitte study of automation in the UK found that while automation and other related technologies have potentially contributed to the loss of over 800,000 lower-skilled jobs, there is equally strong evidence to suggest that it has helped to create nearly 3.5 million new higher-skilled ones in their place (Deloitte, 2015). Automation is a slow process, but it's happening, and the pace of automation varies across different industries. It will bring benefits to both businesses and skilled workers. It's important to note that current jobs won't entirely disappear; many are simply being redefined. Automation will create different specializations of work. Skilled workers for various tasks will be needed to complete varied areas of work in business. It's therefore important to invest in indispensable skills that complement automated work. Today, highly skilled specialists and consultants can be found in nearly every industry on sites like Krop, Shiftgig, Toptal, and 99Designs. Both large and medium-size businesses are continually hiring more flexible workers for short-term tasks. The freelancer workforce is growing at an amazing rate globally, and is showing no signs of slowing down.

Globalization

The explosion of the global trade in services, goods, telecommunications, financial services and technology is creating a new workforce. Globalization is becoming more disruptive. Workers in both developed and developing nations know this. In some countries, people have taken to the streets to protest against the impact of globalization on their jobs. Technology has made a huge impact on this current trend. Advances in technology mean white-collar, office-based workers and business professionals across the world are likely to lose their jobs. 'Ever-faster internet speeds becoming globally more widely available, coupled with the rapidly falling prices of robots will allow workers, for example in the Philippines or China, to remotely provide services to a country like the UK – where the sector accounts for about 80 per cent of the economy,' says Tim Bowler, a business reporter at the BBC (Bowler, 2017).

Globalization mostly affects jobs that can be done anywhere in the world and shipped over the internet. Online platforms that make work easier to ship across the world are levelling the playing field for creative professionals and experts worldwide. The traditional nature of 'work' is disappearing due to the rapid advances in technology. The same trend is also creating new and innovative jobs for highly specialized professionals who have embraced the gig economy. The nature of work is gradually becoming a transactional task exchange. Work is happening everywhere, between people who are hundreds or even thousands of miles away from each other. Even the lines between time of day and work are blurring. Experts who are agile, specialized and capable are taking up contract work from clients from all corners of the world.

Careers of the future

The world of work is disrupted and developed by socioeconomic and geopolitical influences such as advances in technology, increasing globalization and constant change in consumer behaviour. Automation gets a lot of attention, but other drivers of change in the global demand for technology labour include software development and engineering, artificial intelligence, augmented reality, 3D printing and human robots. In an automated economy, tasks that are both indispensable and difficult – perhaps impossible – to automate will stand the test of time. Two examples are healthcare and education, where the need for emotional connection is paramount, making automation unlikely.

In the creative industry (writing, art, design and music) tasks that require originality, innovation and idea generation are less likely to be automated as automated systems may struggle with expressive creativity. People management is also difficult to automate.

In recent times, the demand for roles that weren't even in existence a decade ago is on the rise. Mobile app developers, data miners, social media consultants, content managers and marketing influencers are getting a lot of attention. Even more interesting jobs have been predicted for the future, including artificial intelligence manager, chief data officer and privacy manager.

Ultimately, your choice of career should be determined first and foremost by you – regardless of trends, how you spend your working life should always depend largely on an assessment of your own skills, abilities, personal qualities, interests and expectations of yourself. However, the ways in which the world of work is evolving means you should invest in a career that will stand the test of time. As we have seen, the future is less about jobs, and more about projects, consultancy, contracts and short-term assignments.

Prepare for your future – the skills you need to thrive

The time to embrace constant reinvention as an expert is now. With strategic planning, you can take control of the direction of your future today. Instead of fearing the unpredictable future and what the constant change can do to your career, prepare for it. The increasing preference of businesses to hire independent workers is boosting on-demand talent. Many companies don't hesitate to engage the services of top-end professionals remotely.

> THE FUTURE IS ALREADY HERE. IT'S JUST NOT EVENLY DISTRIBUTED
> **WILLIAM GIBSON**

In the creative industry, where demand for freelancers is soaring, competition for gigs is also becoming fierce. As demand for talent increases, the need for independent professionals to improve their skills and build a personal brand (we will look more closely at personal branding in Chapter 3) to set themselves apart from the competition becomes even more important. Building a successful contract work career requires different skill set. Apart from honing your expertise, and building a marketable and robust portfolio, there are behaviours and skills you can adopt that will prepare you for the future of work and ensure you consistently remain in demand.

Entrepreneur approach to work

The ability to spot opportunities and take initiative is a rare skill that you nevertheless need to thrive in the future as an independent worker. Entrepreneurs see and often seek out opportunities. They apply unconventional tools and approaches to existing challenges. They are agile and can adapt to changing business environments.

As you complete projects, the skill to spot and pick the next best ones will become even more important to your freelance career. When you're a freelancer, you are also, in a fundamental sense, an entrepreneur. Over time, you will build a list of clients, expand your network, and assemble a track record of achievements that are your own. In that sense, freelancing can offer a path to building your own small business. A little entrepreneurial zeal can give you a distinct advantage in your independent work career. Start thinking like a creative entrepreneur. That means instead of just working for hire, you can start creating business assets (personal blog, books, online courses) whose value will increase over time.

Emotional intelligence

Working for yourself is a person-to-person business model. You work to resolve problems and provide solutions for others and their businesses. The way you monitor emotions, both your own and others, and how you use emotional information to guide your thinking and behaviour has a lot to do with how you build business relationships.

The ability to quickly connect with clients and the people you report to about the progress of work is vital emotional intelligence (EI) will be even more important as technology takes over business processes. Improving your EI will allow you to build relationships with others, maintain connection with those you work with and respond in the best way possible to others.

As machines' intelligence improves, they will perform tasks that are better suited to them than humans, such as computation, complex communication, systems thinking, data analysis and logic. Other tasks and functions requiring emotional intelligence, compassion, empathy, creative judgment and discernment will expand and be increasingly valued in the future. Emotional intelligence gives you competitive advantage. Developing a good social relationship with your clients and delivering on the key components of likeability (responsiveness, listening and positivity) helps build lasting business relationships.

Critical thinking and problem solving

Conceptualizing ideas, applying solutions to problems, analysing current solutions, evaluating information, making non-existent connections of knowledge, and analytical reasoning are of immense importance to work. These are desirable skills employers require from full-time workers, part-time employees and on-demand consultants. If you can't think critically, you can't think creatively. And if you can't think creatively, you can't come up with viable solutions to problems for your clients.

Critical thinking and creative thinking go hand in hand. Creative thinking means generating ideas and processes; critical thinking evaluates those thoughts, allowing for rational decisions. Thinking differently can help you solve problems in a completely unexpected way. Critical thinkers make business processes efficient and offer new perspectives to problems. Improve how you think and give yourself the best possible chance to thrive in the future.

Negotiation

Every independent worker needs to master and practise the art of negotiation. It's a priceless skill that has a huge impact on your income. Negotiating a fair rate and client relationship for your work is a critical competency. This applies to negotiating for pricing or project scope. To compete and win projects or clients, you should stick to the basic rule of freelancer negotiation; start with a goal in mind, know what you are worth (establish your value), research the client, negotiate more than money (think assignment scope, status updates, deadlines), be flexible and open to alternative arrangements valuable to you in the future (equity, referrals, future business or even attribution), look beyond the price and negotiate with the future in mind. In any negotiation, focus on the long term. Your goal should be multiple repeat clients. Build better relationships with clients.

To improve your odds of success in any negotiation:

- Think about what you want or need from an outcome.
- Anticipate the other party's likely approach and perspective.
- Be very clear about your unique benefits. Sell the benefits of your service to the prospective client.
- Don't feel pressured to accept an offer. If you can, secure an initial agreement before you start negotiating. For example, 'If we can agree on the details, would you be happy to go ahead?'

Networking

Marketing yourself and your service like any other company is a huge booster for your career as an independent worker (we will talk about personal branding in Chapter 3). Networking builds relationships. Those relationships build connections, and connections build sales. The basic form of networking (attending relevant conferences, industry events and meet-ups) is great for your career. Networking, both online and offline, increases your job offers, and strengthen relationships for future work. Meeting other freelancers at co-working spaces and meet-ups opens you up to new opportunities. You are more likely to receive business referrals from your network than through cold contacts.

Pitching clients, following up, staying in touch and maintaining contact with existing clients even after delivering work are important skills you should nurture. Your portfolio (a combination of your unique approach and your best work) alone may not be able to attract as many clients as you would want, as both individuals and employees consistently do business with the people they know already. Refining your networking skills can go a long way for you as a gig worker. It's a valuable process for your long-term success.

Adaptability

The rapid change of business trends demands an agile and adaptable workforce. The workplaces of tomorrow will be more flexible, collaborative and mobile. The future world of work will soon become 'the survival of the most adaptable' at any point in time. Change, constant improvement and greater efficiency are all sought after and encouraged in many industries. Business transformation is never-ending, so embrace change and learn to thrive in an ambiguous environment. Adaptability allows you to make the most of new circumstances and stay on top of current situations. The ability to adapt as the world of work changes and new business processes emerge in a fast-paced digital will become crucial to your success. Employers expect short-term workers to have a better understanding of business processes in their fields. Clients expect on-demand talent they hire to meet varying, changing demands.

Apart from knowing how to get your work done, you should be able to collaborate, communicate well with your clients with the right tools, and adjust to changing demands that fall within the project scope. Whatever your industry of work, your success will depend on your ability to harness and embrace the power of change. Practise being adaptable and flexible in your approach to work. You will profit from it both in your own development of additional skills as well as in your career.

Building a successful portfolio career

Until recently, employers were more than happy to work with employees for as long as they wanted. They valued employees with strong and unique exper-tise much more than people with cross-sector experience in many industries. Business modes have changed, and they keep changing. Today, businesses value flexibil-ity. Location independent work is becoming increasingly popular in many industries. People are increasingly embracing the multi-ple short jobs approach to work. Pan Pan, Founder and Managing

> A CAREER IS A PORTFOLIO OF PROJECTS THAT TEACH YOU NEW SKILLS, GAIN YOU NEW EXPERTISE, DEVELOP NEW CAPABILITIES, GROW YOUR COLLEAGUE SET, AND CONSTANTLY REINVENT YOU AS A BRAND
> **TOM PETERS**

Partner of Pantera Ventures, argues that your success depends on your ability to learn relevant new skills every now and then, to be indispensable in the new world of work. 'The new-economy requires people to not just learn new skills as they age, but to moni-tor the market for new opportunities,' she says (Pan, 2015). The fundamental idea of a 'portfolio' approach to your career is to think of work not as a single, stable, secured role at a single location, but as a set of skills and interests that define who you are and what you do. Instead of identifying with a single job description, you build your professional life as a portfolio of accomplishments, skills and abilities. A portfolio mind-set and career can easily make you a well-rounded person and set you up for success in an ever-changing work economy. The more specific your skill set and experience, the more valuable your portfolio will be.

Your portfolio should showcase your experience in your industry. As a general rule, on-demand workers should not work for free, but there is an exception. If you genuinely believe that a few hours of your time will bring long-term real exposure and subsequently lead to the acquisition of clients, you can accept to work for equity, attri-bution or testimonial. If you want to, peg your portfolio as a writer, get published on Medium as a writer in a particular niche. Submit your pieces to popular magazines or publications for consideration. Opportunities may be hard to find in the beginning. The easiest and quickest solution to getting a public online portfolio, whilst you consider a robust portfolio sometime soon, is an up-to-date LinkedIn profile. There's more to a LinkedIn profile than just listing your previous jobs. Get it right if you already have one. The profiles that appeal to prospective clients are significantly different. It will pay to revamp it now. Log into your LinkedIn profile and visit the 'edit profile' page to make the following change, if you have not done so already:

- Use your best professional picture. This simple change can increase your page views. While you're at it, you should consider finally adding a cover photo to your profile.

- Craft a concise valued-centred headline to define who you are in the minds of prospective clients. Example: 'Helping small businesses build customer-friendly websites'.

- Your LinkedIn profile is searchable, so use every field to your advantage. Don't just list past jobs – also focus on your accomplishments. Describe your best work that is relevant to your skill.

- Highlight the kind of work you enjoy most and the type of work you are looking for in the future.

- If you are looking to attract clients, show why every project you worked on or every team you worked with needed you.

- In the summary section, you should be brief and to the point about what you do and want. Remember to include key words in your summary – these are words that a prospective client might type in when looking for a suitable gig consultant.

- Use the publishing platform to share educational content. By publishing content, you can provide value to your network and be seen as an expert.

- And when you are ready to go beyond LinkedIn, tools like Wix, SquareSpace, and About.me are great options for building a simple and professional public portfolio.

If the thought of settling on one industry and climbing the career ladder doesn't feel like a goal you can commit to, a portfolio career could be for you. A portfolio career can be the perfect manifestation of who you are as a whole person, and give you the freedom, flexibility and autonomy to increase your workflow accordingly.

Exercise: How to figure out the right skill to pursue

Where should you focus your efforts to build a successful portfolio career? Think about these questions to help you figure out the right skill you need to develop or build to start and create a successful career in the gig the gig economy:

- What do you want to be known for professionally?
- If you had the right skill, what choice of career would you enjoy doing and why?
- What would you do if you had time to pursue a personal passion project?
- How far are you on the path to excellence in your current field?
- What steps can you take to becoming an expert in your niche and how long will it take you if you are learning a new skill?
- What are your motivations, needs and skills, and what are you willing to do or give up to find that fulfilling opportunity?
- What do you want to get really good at doing?
- What motivates you and what bores you?
- When was the last time you massively over-delivered on a task or project? What was it and why did you work so hard at it?
- Out of all your current work roles, what would you gladly do for free?

Once you're done answering these questions, take a close look at your answers. You may find clear-cut patterns that can point you in the right direction. Don't hesitate to share your answers with a mentor, friend or a colleague. An objective eye can help you see patterns you may be missing. Knowing what you value, what you enjoy doing, and what you want to be known for in the next decade is a great way to get started honing in on what you want from your career. Think about the possibilities, and how your current skills can combine with your passions to help you build the career that can make you an expert.

Reinvent your career

The independent work revolution is upon us, and it has only just begun. The changing economy is enabling professionals around the world to share their skills and expertise with businesses from around the world. Opportunities for gig work are increasing fast. If flexibility and freedom are important to how you work, now is the time to embrace the gig economy.

Work meant loyalty to a single company in the past. For millions of people today, on-demand work is emerging as the ideal lifestyle. People are increasingly designing their careers to adapt to their diverse, ever-changing ambitions and interests. It's now easier to jump to the next best career without difficulty. Working life is gradually moving towards a series of continuous projects. Choose to work on projects that bring out the best in you. Reinvention is a career shift during which you close one chapter and step into a new one. In the past, when people achieved job or career stability, they despised change. Today, change is an important part of stability. You can only achieve career stability in many industries by embracing change as a continuous part of work.

To survive and thrive in any career, you have to redefine and reinvent yourself and your career continuously. Many people reinvent themselves because they get tired of their old life or career. Others are forced into reinvention because their job goes away or some other life event requires them to start over in a new situation. For millions of people today, reinvention is a deliberate career choice. Whatever reinvention means to you, it can work for your particular situation.

According to CareerBuilder's 2017 forecast, more than half of employers are seeking contract workers, a 47 per cent increase from the previous year (Braun, 2017). You have options when you decide to pursue life as a gig worker. Employees are consistently embracing short-term work. There are opportunities for you. Whatever your industry, there are online marketplaces out there to help you find work. You don't even have to resign from your current job immediately to pursue independent work. You can take on part-time gigs to build your portfolio whilst you prepare for life as a full-time independent consultant. You can also dive right into freelance work by speaking to your employer about moving to a part-time role, giving you some free time to build up your new career. The time to reinvent your career as an independent consultant is now. If you long for more freedom and flexibility and are willing to work for it, your life will never be the same.

The need for change often depends on your perspective – fear of the unknown versus growth opportunity. Choose to demand more of yourself and build the life you have always wanted. Don't get stuck in a single, unfulfilling pursuit. Begin to create a body of work. Keep building and honing your skills to complement your core skill.

Career assessment

Loving what you do is a wonderful thing. You can improve your finances and also get the added reward of feeling fulfilled, accomplished and satisfied each time you take on a new task or project. You enjoy your time at work. When in doubt about your next career option, take time and assess your skills.

To take charge of the rest of your work life, start listing all your areas of competence and narrow down on a few you can consider and pursue. A simple way to find out the skills you should consider is to review the jobs and responsibilities on your current CV. Which ones did you enjoy doing? Which tasks were your favourite parts about each job? Take note of them. This simple exercise can help you find out a few things that excite you. It can help you figure out what you need to learn or already know in order to get to your ultimate goal of building a portfolio career.

The prospect of building a successful independent career depends on what you are good at. Your strengths are what make you come alive and energize you. Think about the work you do that brings out the best in you. You lose track of time, and are deeply engaged when working on a task you a passionate about. What makes you excited to go to work the next day? It's not necessarily about the job, but the different things you do whilst at work. These are clues that can help you explore your strengths, passions and interests when you finally make a decision to work for yourself. Focus more on your most valued talents and the skills you have acquired through your work experience. They can help you choose the right tasks, projects and gigs that would add meaning to your career and life.

Examine your current abilities, skills and interests at your current role and find out where your interests intersect. Take note of the times when you are in complete control of tasks. These moments are clues to what your strengths are. Concentrate on the skills you're interested in using and work out where and how you can deploy them when you choose to work for yourself. Sometimes, what you want to focus on in the future may not necessarily be what you are good at but what you really want to do. In that case, you can improve those skills. Evaluate your specific background in the light of your new career choice. If you have already decided on how to pitch yourself as an expert, then reformat your accomplishments and skills to make them relevant to future prospects. You can quickly take an inventory of your career by writing down what you like and don't like about your current work or projects you have done. It's easier to make that huge career transition knowing that you are preparing yourself for something you truly enjoy.

Career assessment exercise

A career change is a big decision. One of the benefits of conducting an assessment is that it allows you to identify and address potential problems before they happen. It gives you the opportunity to know exactly what you expect of yourself now and in the future. It can also help you to set realistic and measurable goals, whether that means taking on new projects in your current career, enhancing your skill set or shifting into a new career in a completely new industry. This clarity can help you gain control of your life.

Working in a fulfilling career can dramatically increase your happiness and self-confidence, and improve your total well-being. The following questions can help you take action in the right direction when you are ready to move in your professional life. Analyse your answers and look for clues to guide your decision:

- What is the one thing I am really good at?
- What do I really want to get out of life?
- How much control do I have over my schedule?
- What activities are rewarding to me at work?
- What do I love to do most at work?
- What am I known for?
- Is my current job helping me achieve my long-term goals?
- Do I have the skills to work in a new area of interest?
- Do my skills match rising changes in how work is done and delivered?

Career transition

Using the questions in the career assessment exercise above as a guide, construct an image in your mind about your ideal future and what you expect from yourself. Take time to imagine different career options you can pursue. Think about a variety of possible lifestyles and which one best describes what you want now and in the future. Use the different images of yourself in the future to guide your early career decisions. The idea is to get a sense of the lifestyle you want and how to get it. If thinking about any particular career lifestyle makes you excited to pursue that path, it's a good match. It's a starting point to building something meaningful.

Take it a step further and write out your idealized, perfect career in detail. Describe your ideal self in a journal, including your skills, abilities, prospective clients and even what your daily plan could look like. Once you know what you want your ideal lifestyle to look like, you can begin to adjust your present life and make decisions to get closer to the perfect career. If you take the exercise seriously, you will begin to make conscious decisions that can improve your current skills, and change how you spend your time and what to focus on, to get the life you want. Even if you don't make a drastic change in your career, you will learn more about yourself in the process.

A dream lifestyle provides you with the opportunity to be your best self. It helps you discover potential paths previously hidden from your planning process. This exercise can help you examine your current life and your future goals, and think unconventionally about how to make your life awesome. You can make that important career transition to be your best self without regrets. And that requires personal sacrifice. In his free manifesto 'A brief guide to world domination' (2018), Chris Guillebeau, author of *The Art of Non-Conformity*, says, 'You have to be able to devote significant time to improving your skills. You don't just want to be good enough; you want to be remarkable. What this means is different for everyone – some people are able to pursue world domination in their off hours, while others will need more time.'

The career transition exercise can help you achieve your long-term career goals and focus on what's important to you in the future. In the short run it will help you take actionable steps like improving your skills to thrive and do better in the future when you are ready to embrace life as an independent consultant. When you work towards building your dream career, you will do work you enjoy and have more time and energy for fun activities you like to do.

How to use an information interview to figure out a career path

One of the best ways to find everything you need to know about a particular career path is to conduct an informal interview people who are working in that field.

When you're interviewing for information, you're attempting to discover everything about their job. There's an untapped potential in simple curiosity. Often, the most current and genuine information about a career field is not available online. You can easily find the right people to interview on LinkedIn if you are still looking for people to contact. You can also ask the right people in your network to reach out to the contacts you want to interview on your behalf. Once the connection is established, reach out and make the purpose of the interview clear, in advance.

Ideas on how to write your first email

- Keep the email short. State who you are, and what the connection is. For example, a friend recommended them to you.
- Let them know you are not looking for a job or referral.
- Do not include a CV. The interview is strictly about them and what they do.
- Request 30 minutes of their time to ask a few questions. You can suggest a date and let them know you are open to other dates suitable to them.
- Thank them for their time.

Once they accept your request for an interview, do your research and get to know them. Read about them on their company website, personal websites, blogs and social media accounts.

Questions to ask

Think about the information you want from them and ask your questions accordingly. Focus on open-ended questions that allow them to talk about themselves instead of closed-ended ones. Example:

- How did you choose your present career path?
- How did you get started?
- What does your typical day look like?
- What are the important lessons you have learned so far?
- What are the most rewarding and challenging thing about working in this industry?

- What do you wish someone would have told you before going into this field?

- Who else do you think I should speak to?

Answers to these questions should help you understand whether you would like to spend your day doing the same thing. After the interview, immediately send an email thanking the person for his or her time. After your interview, you can experiment with your top four career options in a small way part-time to find out which one you would love doing and can bring you the fulfilment you need. If you have a lot of experience in your current job, it's even easier to pitch yourself as an expert or consultant in the future. If you don't have the skill for an option that could bring you personal satisfaction, learn it. Retraining can help you become who you want to be. Make time for it after work to improve your skills. After your experiment, you can make a decision about your current job. You can hand in your notice if you have enough information about your next career and its prospects. Make sure all the necessary financial arrangement are in place to take care of yourself and your family during the transition when you will not have regular income.

Key takeaways

- The world of work is wide open to revolutionary, transformational developments but you are more than capable of remaining indispensable to employers.

- Despite the many challenges of automation and its impact on the global workforce, jobs won't entirely disappear; many will simply be redefined.

- It pays to stay flexible and open to new opportunities while continuing to hone your existing skills.

- In an ever-changing work environment, pitching yourself as an expert in your industry can put you ahead of other professionals.

- A career that makes it easy to work as consultant for a number of companies simultaneously rather than working for one big corporation is a unique way to diversify your source of income.

- Work as a series of fulfilling experiences will allow you to thrive in your industry and still earn money, but be happier and more intellectually fulfilled, and with infinitely more flexibility. Think of every new experience as contributing to the portfolio of work you're building – not for a single employer or client.

- As an expert in your field, think ahead and manage around this: be clear on what specific outcomes you're shooting for, and actively seek ones that fit this profile.

- The most important skills you need to stay relevant in the future are an entrepreneurial approach to work, emotional intelligence, negotiation skills, the ability to make better connections and build relationships, critical thinking and adaptability.

References

Bowler, T (2017) Will globalisation take away your job? 1/2 [Online] www.bbc.co.uk/news/business-38600270

Braun, K (2017) Temporary hiring trends in 2017 and beyond, 26/1 [Online] https://resources.careerbuilder.com/staffing/temporary-hiring-trends-in-2017-and-beyond

Deloitte (2015) From brawn to brains: The impact of technology on jobs in the UK [Online] www2.deloitte.com/content/dam/Deloitte/uk/Documents/Growth/deloitte-uk-insights-from-brawns-to-brain.pdf

Gibson, W (2003) *The Economist*, 4 December.

Guillebeau, C (2018) A brief guide to world domination [Online] chrisguillebeau.com

Pan Pan (2015) Why you should build a portfolio career, 24/8 [Online] knowledge.insead.edu/blog/insead-blog/why-you-should-build-a-portfolio-career-4221

Price Waterhouse Coopers (2017) Press room, 3/2017 [Online] pwc.blogs.com/press_room/2017/03/up-to-30-of-existing-uk-jobs-could-be-impacted-by-automation-by-early-2030s-but-this-should-be-offse.html

Seagal, C (2016) Will jobs exist in 2050? 13/10 [Online] www.theguardian.com/careers/2016/oct/13/will-jobs-exist-in-2050

03
How to build your independent brand and strengthen your reputation as a gig worker

Personal brand is how people perceive you; how they'd describe you – similar to how you would describe a famous person or company. You may be committed to one employer, but a simple change of mindset can make all the difference for your career.

Even if you're a full-time employee, you can still invest in your personal brand. In this chapter we

> **BRAND YOURSELF FOR THE CAREER YOU WANT, NOT THE JOB YOU HAVE**
> **DAN SCHAWBEL**

will discuss why personal branding is important for your success as a freelancer, how to succeed as a business of one, what to do to harness online media to grow your personal brand and how your reputation can make or break your business.

Building a personal brand

Branding is an important goal, not just for Fortune 100 companies but also for individuals who have pitched themselves as experts, consultants or freelancers. Dorie Clark explains in her book, *Stand*

Out: How to find your breakthrough idea and build a following around it, 'In today's competitive economy, it's not enough to simply do your job well. Developing a personal brand as expert attracts people who want to hire you, do business with you and your company, and spread your ideas. It's the ultimate form of career insurance' (Clark, 2015). Dorie couldn't have explained it any better. The growing need for on-demand workforce globally means one thing for independent workers: competition for clients. Self-marketing is now more important than ever. As competition for business, contracts, clients and customers become fierce, branding has become a professional requirement. Branding is key to the success of any on-demand worker.

Your brand is something you will have to manage online, offline, in your chosen industry and on social media. Consistency is key. Today, branding yourself might be easier than ever, but it's harder to stand out and win clients if you don't offer something different, unique, more valuable and authentic. But the gig economy era holds limitless opportunities for committed experts. If you are an authentic and passionate brand, you are in control. You choose your clients. Pitching yourself as a brand is one of the keys to reinventing yourself from just another gig worker to a highly demanded independent contractor. Whether you're hoping for a promotion, trying to land a big client or just starting out as a freelancer, one thing is certain: you have to stand out. You have to learn how to speak out on your own behalf. Every professional, expert or consultant in any industry is a brand. Regardless of your chosen profession, you are a 'business of one' and your success depends on your personal brand. To succeed or be guarantee repeat business in any professional endeavour, it's crucial to make your unique value memorable.

Define your goals

Building a memorable personal brand is centred around these key questions: Who are you? What would you like to achieve, and for what purpose? If you are able to figure out the best answers, you will have a compelling brand.

Defining personal goals can set you up for success when you are ready to redefine your role in the world of work. You should have a goal in mind at any point of your career. Building the best 'brand of you' requires understanding and defining both short-term and long-term goals. Branding is built over time; it's therefore important to identify and align your brand with your goals. The first step to creating a successful independent brand is to organize your thoughts and create your personal brand vision for the next few years.

What are you great at? What are you most excited about achieving in your career in the next year or next five years? Do you want to climb the uncertain corporate ladder, or would you rather enhance your expertise and offer your service to multiple clients? What is the one thing you want your audience or prospective clients to take away when they come across your profile, portfolio or when you make your first contact? What brand are you seeking to build? Your answers to these important career questions are crucial to your success.

Goal-setting exercise

What is the big picture of what you want to accomplish as an expert? This simple exercise is an important step that can help you achieve your career goals.

1 Using a journal for record keeping purposes, write down everything you want to achieve in the next five and ten years.

2 Separate your goals into career, professional development, financial, family, health and leisure. There is no limit to the number of broad categories you can include on your list.

3 For each category, give it a timeline. Some categories will be more pressing than others. Arrange them based on importance. You can focus on the next 12 months, five years and ten years from now depending on the most important category you want to achieve in the shortest time possible.

4 Use the SMART (specific, measurable, attainable, realistic and time-bound) goal format for each of your categories, especially

for the short-term goals you choose. For example, to change careers in the next 12 months, list actions you need to take every week, and every month, to get you closer to that goal. Items on that list could be: structure LinkedIn profile, identify the one skill you need to position yourself as an expert (the one skill if developed that would have the greatest impact on your career), buy a domain, build a personal website, create a marketing message, build other social profiles, take a career reinvention course, ask current employer to repurpose responsibility as a consultant, and finally submit letter of resignation as a full-time worker.

5 Group your goals into smaller and easy to achieve milestones. The more detailed you can be in outlining your activities, the better.

6 Plan your next month, week by week, or the next 12 months, month by month. For each week, or month, list two or three activities that you must accomplish. Commit time to the list and make plans to achieve them. It's the only way to achieve any important goal in life.

7 To help you achieve your goals, write them on sticky notes and place them at places where you can remind yourself daily to take action. This can help you review and measure them daily or weekly.

A business of one

Career-conscious go-getters strive for a work life available only through a location-independent career lifestyle. To evolve with the new world of work, you have to adapt at becoming responsible for your career. Think of yourself as a 'business of one', capable of working with multiple clients. Creating your own dream job and career is the best approach to get the life you want. To take your career towards a desired future, you have be your own boss – controlling your career, finding and seizing the right opportunities, and building an amazing portfolio in the process.

Think of it this way: your skills, experience and personal traits that make you who you are don't disappear if you lose your job, or if your employer goes bankrupt. Your life doesn't stop if your immediate boss quits. Your unique skills are yours, and no one can ever take them away from you. The sooner you realize how useful you are to yourself and your career, the better for your future prospects. 'Think of your career as a series of experiences,' says Lenny Mendonca, Senior Partner at McKinsey. Your freelancer career is a portfolio of your past work. You can only get better with time.

Think like an entrepreneur

Successful independent consultants are proactive. To succeed as a gig worker, you should think like an entrepreneur. The entrepreneurial mindset is characterized by initiative, adventure, risk and perseverance. One thing that links the most successful on-demand workers in all industries is that they take a proactive approach to managing their careers. People who are ahead of the game in the gig economy don't wait for a career emergency to reinvent themselves or update their portfolio. Take an innovative approach to your career and do more than what an average person will do.

When you are selling your services to perspective clients, you are selling yourself. You are building a 'brand of you' that can stand the test of time. Turning your talent into a branded business that others trust is an important step in your career. Over the next decade, on-demand workers will be in high demand in many industries. If you intend to win client business today, tomorrow, and well into the future, you need to focus on building your unique portfolio. It's the only way to successfully compete with established companies for clients.

People and businesses will choose to work with you because of your past, or because they've worked with you and trust that you will deliver on your promises. Becoming credible in your chosen career is the result of working consistently overtime to make a huge difference to your audience and clients. As with any new businesses, building a successful 'business of one' takes time and planning.

Harnessing online media

Marketing experts agree that how you present yourself online is the 21st century equivalent of your first meeting with a customer. Seth Godin, Tim Ferriss, Gary Vaynerchuk, Tony Robbins are all larger-than-life characters who own their spaces both online and offline. Think about your favourite influencers or thought leaders. What makes them recognizable to you? It could be their personality, their businesses, what they teach or write about, or a combination of all three. It's never too late to build an influential career that can stand the test of time.

Using online media platforms might be the most efficient way to self-promote your speciality to the public. You get maximum exposure for a relatively small amount of investment of time and money. Think about it this way: if you schedule time to network one-on-one with a prospective client over lunch, you spend one hour making an impression on one person. But if you write a relevant, educational and timeless blog post, you could spend two to three hours writing to make an impression on thousands of people.

Everything you do, say, or share online or offline is gradually forming your personal brand. Your personal brand has a lot to do with your professional reputation, so take it seriously – what does your current identity reveal about you? Make no mistake, anyone who wants to work with you or hire you on contract to solve a problem in their business is likely to Google you, so you should audit yourself online regularly. Take note of profile consistency, colours and social media handles. Right now, go to google.com and type your name into the search and witness what the world's most popular search engine shows about you to the world. If you are surprised or embarrassed by the results, try to do something about it. Every piece of content (text, images, videos) you have published online in the past can be managed. Your reputation must be built in the best way possible to reflect the image you expect of yourself. Google yourself regularly and make a conscious effort to influence what Google reveals about you by publishing content you expect others to see. You can use Klout to help you measure how influential you are in your area of expertise, and find out how successful influencers grow their audience.

Show your work

Personal branding gives you the competitive edge to connect with relevant people in your industry. Blogging is one the best and cheapest ways to have a voice online. A blog is a hub for your advice, thoughts and opinions on a niche topic. For the last three years, I have consistently published posts on how to be productive and work better on Medium.com. In the past year online publications like Business Insider, Huffington Post, Thought Catalog, Inc. Magazine, Quartz and CNBC reached out to republish some of my content on Medium. And that opened a lot of opportunities for my career as a writer. You can easily start a blog by going to any one of these leading hosted blogging platforms and follow the instructions for setting up your account: medium.com, wordpress.com or wix.com.

Apart from blogging, you can create opportunities to meet and engage with others through speaking at events, and partnering with others to host events, meetings, podcasts and web conferences. You can start part-time whilst you are preparing to reinvent your full-time independent contracting career. If you are currently employed, familiarize yourself with your company's blogging policy and make sure you are not breaking any rules. Separate your personal branding efforts from your company's. Consider blogging about your expertise and the industry but not your employer.

Your posts should be focused on your specialized competencies, the concerns, problems and frustrations of your target audience and your unique way of delivering value to your audience. People expect your blog to reveal your personality, so provide a small window into your world as well.

It takes time to grow your brand and build the right relationships; focus on delivering amazing educational content. Strong brands and personalities take time to build. The key is to maintain a career momentum. Don't stop reinventing yourself. Not every action will be perfect. It takes time to get the results you want, so don't stop because you are not getting results. Consistency will eventually pay. As your career develops, and you improve your brand, review your goals, skills and competencies. Add to it to serve your audience and clients better. Evolving your brand means thinking of new ways to deliver on your personal brand promise.

You are your reputation

Reputation is as important as your brand in the gig economy. Your brand is how you present yourself to others or clients. You control and decide how you represent your brand. It's the accumulation of your actions overtime. A great reputation is a gig worker's best advocate.

> YOUR REPUTATION IS IN THE HANDS OF OTHERS. THAT'S WHAT THE REPUTATION IS. YOU CAN'T CONTROL THAT. THE ONLY THING YOU CAN CONTROL IS YOUR CHARACTER
>
> **WAYNE DYER**

Everyone prefers to work with people with solid reputations. People they can trust. And those with credibility. It takes time to build a great career as an on-demand worker. It's a culmination of years of consistent work and effort. The good news is, you can establish yourself after working with a few clients. And that will be a great foundation to build your career even further.

The long-term reputation that guarantees work depends on your work ethics and relationships with clients as your grow. Take client relationships seriously. Establish a good relationship with every business or client you choose to work with. It can win more work for you in the future. If your clients don't feel comfortable referring you to others, something is wrong. Seek feedback from your clients to improve how you work.

And don't take common courtesy and transparency for granted. Build your reputation as an independent contractor who over delivers on promises. It's better to under-promise and go the extra mile to deliver great client satisfaction. Every little action matters when you want to be recognized as an authority in your niche.

Your reputation can be affected by a number of factors, including your portfolio, work habits, testimonials, completed projects, others' opinion about you, and your authority in your industry. A positive reputation attracts clients.

Key takeaways

- Building a strong brand is the only way to stand out.

- Define your goals right from the beginning.

- Know your brand voice and stay consistent to strengthen your reputation.

- Get social to create a public presence. Creating awareness about your expertise is the best thing you can do as an independent gig worker.

- A blog is a great way to expand your brand statement. Create and share educative content that reinforces your brand and promotes your skill.

- A great brand confirms credibility. Focus on building a reputation. This takes time. Be professional.

References

Clark, D (2015) *Stand Out: How to find your breakthrough idea and build a following around it* [Online] www.goodreads.com/author/quotes/6467972.Dorie_Clark

Karen Kang, Branding Pays: The Five-Step System to Reinvent Your Personal Brand 1/2013 [Online] www.amazon.com/BrandingPays-Five-Step-System-Reinvent-Personal-ebook/dp/B00BVDLT2S

04
Finding work in the gig economy

Differentiation makes a lot of difference for freelancers who seek new challenges and clients. In this chapter we'll look at actions you should take to help you find work, and discuss why you should pursue a purpose-driven career. We'll also consider the importance of positioning as a gig worker, the value of limited free work, how to find your first client, why you should make real connections offline, why creating your own project is one of the best approaches to working for yourself, and will finish the chapter by seeing why it's important to partner with other freelancers.

Positioning

Thriving as an independent worker is all about positioning. It's about communicating the right message to potential clients. A portfolio is one of the best ways to position yourself in the best way possible to attract clients. Traditionally, a portfolio has been a collection of your work to spark interest from potential clients. To get the best work, and even get prospective clients to contact you, you need to rethink the value of your portfolio. It needs to display the quality of your work and convey the necessary information businesses will find useful in making a decision to work with you. A portfolio that answers questions will get you hired, a portfolio that raises questions about your competencies won't get you far. Don't just list your skills; share the problems you solved for previous clients or former employer. Use testimonials to back up your skills.

When you do a good job at positioning yourself, you will stand out and your value will be obvious to clients. Show why you are different from others, and why you are the best person for the job.

Building a purpose-driven career

There are many things you could do with your career, but the people who are most successful have found a combination of fulfilment, money and flow (the mental state where your best work emerges without struggle). Choose to work on projects that fulfil a higher purpose. Passion will give you every reason to fulfil your dreams. Freelancing can take up a lot of your productive time, so it's imperative to work projects that bring out the best in you. Yes you need work to pay the bills, but work is more than a means of earning a living. If you don't enjoy what do, chances are you will be miserable, even if you work for yourself. Having purpose gives you the confidence to turn down projects that may stress you or go against your moral code. Purposeful independent work gives you the resilience and strength for the ups and downs of self-employment. Pursuing career fulfilment takes time. It takes practice. It's a process, not a destination. Discovering what you care about, gaining the reputation for what you do, and building career capital takes a little bit of time, but it's worth it.

> IT IS IMPOSSIBLE TO HAVE A GREAT LIFE UNLESS IT IS A MEANINGFUL LIFE. AND IT IS VERY DIFFICULT TO HAVE A MEANINGFUL LIFE WITHOUT MEANINGFUL WORK
> **JIM COLLINS**

Giving limited free advice

Free work has a bad reputation. According to Jeff Goins, author of *Real Artists Don't Starve,* 'Working for free is not the "opportunity" we often think it is. Opportunity doesn't pay the bills' (2017).

Jeff argues that starving artists work for free and that thriving artists know what they are worth. But for many independent workers who are just starting out, it can be the necessary step to gaining valuable exposure, building an attractive portfolio, making connections, getting referrals and testimonials. Seth Godin, an influential business blogger, and author of eighteen international bestsellers, once said, 'And in some settings, this makes perfect sense. You might be making a contribution to a cause you care about, or, more likely, honing your craft at the same time that you get credibility and attention for your work.'

Offering free advice or solving a minor problem for potential clients for free may not be ideal, but it can open up new opportunities. This approach does not apply in every industry, but you can use it different ways, including free giveaways, offers, discounts, free trials and downloads to get exposure. Instead of directing people to your website to read about your services and what you can do, why not provide something of value they can try for a few minutes, hours or days. You can start off by offering free services to charities or non-profit organizations. Carefully selected free projects will help those in need of assistance and improve your collection of past work. In exchange, you can request referrals and testimonials from your clients. Referrals are your best friend when you start pursuing an independent work career. On-demand work is a career path built on referrals.

If you start a blog in your industry to educate your audience for free, you will attract targeted clients in your industry. HubSpot, an inbound marketing and sales platform, maintains a robust blog that educates prospective customers through blog posts and eBooks. Neil Patel, an influential marketer, also publishes free valuable blog posts and eBooks to help his audience learning the fundamentals of marketing. Help a few people solve their problems. If someone is interested in something you offer for free, there is chance they could pay you for it in the future. Marketers use this approach to attract prospective customers before they pitch them their products. When someone gets to know you, it's easier for them to like you and subsequently trust you enough to buy from you or choose you to work on a project. You can build meaningful relationships with clients through this method. On your website, when you give away a free download, educational industry checklist, training exercise or a report, exchange this content for email addresses and registration information. It can take time to make money when you choose to offer your service for free, but the payoff can be worth it. Even if you don't win an organization's business in the future, you've at least built something portfolio-worthy, or achieved something worth mentioning to future clients.

Securing your first client

Securing your first client can be intimidating. Don't think about getting dozens of clients you can work with – focus on winning just one client and then scale from there. Use the following structure to develop a great proposal that will successfully solve a prospective client's problem:

- **Problem identified** – The client's problem you intend to solve, their needs, objectives and goals. State how the problem affects their bottom line profitability, and what you can do about it.

- **Recommended solution** – The solution you are offering, strategy to solve, your plan of action and why you are uniquely positioned to solve that specific problem. In some cases, you can provide the solution to win future business.

- **Fee and project schedule** – If you are pitching based on how you intend to solve the problem, instead of offering the solution include your timelines, fee structure, what will it cost, when payment is due and how soon you can deliver on your promise.

Be patient when you start submitting proposals. It can take a dozen proposals to win your first client. Just keep trying and iterate your proposal, keep rethinking your strategy and solution for each client. Career transitions take time. After serving a few clients your strategy for finding new clients will get better. As you grow, build structures and business systems to take care of the routines.

The first gig exercise

This simple exercise can help you narrow down to focus on the few things you should be doing to land your first gig:

- Get a journal and write down all the things you do well. Leave nothing out. List everything you can do that can be marketed. Be honest with yourself and don't waste your own time. I suggest that you spend no more than an hour trying to figure this out. Take a break and come back to it if you can. Some things will occur to you when your brain is in a relaxed mode.

- Return to the list and start picking those items that you can actively monetize. What do you think people will be willing to pay for on that list? What can you do easily and get paid for it? Is there anything on that list that people currently pay for as a service provided by other freelancers or businesses?

- Select just one thing on your list you would like to try and monetize. It could be anything: writing, editing, website design, photography, social media consulting, running errands, making deliveries, part-time driving, online research, fitness instructor, renting extra space, care giving, tutoring, event planning, etc. Anything you can do right now and get paid for it.

- Write just one sentence that describes how you want to pitch yourself. Example, 'I am a freelancer and I create amazing Facebook pages', or 'I design websites for new entrepreneurs.' This is an important step because a description of yourself is important for finding gigs. It's the headline you need to present yourself to your audience or prospective clients. Make it consistent across your online platforms.

- Who will you target? Who could possibly buy from you or hire your service? Answers to these questions can help you attract the right clients. They will also help you direct your efforts at the right gig platforms.

- Once you know whom to target, work on a visibility plan to attract your very first client. Who needs to know who you are and what you are great at? In most cases there are online niche platforms you can use to find prospective clients (we will discuss online platforms for finding work in Chapter 10).

The biggest hurdle to becoming a full-time gig worker is finding your very first client. It might seem overwhelming, but with the right attitude, perseverance and focus, you'll be up and running in no time.

Making it easier for clients to come to you

One of the greatest challenges for new contract workers is finding clients. Every freelancer's journey begins with that important search for clients. Share your work on LinkedIn, Medium and on your own blog. Add sharing features that allow people to share your free resources with their audience. Use LinkedIn to share even more niche resources with other business professionals. Build relationships online and offline and consistently demonstrate your value to your audience and clients.

Go a step further once you start sharing your work. Don't just wait for businesses to come to you – make it easy for them to find your work in so many different places that they'll have no choice but to reach out. 'Now that I've built a sizeable audience, I earn a majority of my income through affiliate marketing, advertising space, and managing content for a few other websites,' says Michelle Schroeder, personal finance blogger and freelance strategy consultant, in an interview with Forbes (Robinson, 2016). Schroeder uses her MBA in finance to write content for finance-related websites.

Brandon Seymour, a content marketing SEO and conversion optimization consultant, uses the same content marketing approach to attract clients. Seymour leverages sites like Moz, Search Engine Journal, and others to build authority. 'One article in particular led to connections that brought in about $40,000 in revenue over the course of one year,' he said, in the same interview with Robinson.

Build something worth sharing in your industry. Create content worth republishing by industry leaders or leading publishers in your niche. In recent times, it's one of the best ways you can get discovered. People want proof that you can deliver on your promises.

Scheduling time to connect

The best way to find quality clients and build better relationships for the future is to find and attend niche conferences, events, meetups and networking events. Make it easier for companies to engage your services. Go to any and every relevant networking event that matches your interests, and simply tell people what you do and what you've done.

Many networking events can be found online. In small towns, relevant events happen occasionally, so look out for them and use them to your advantage. Even if you don't win clients right away at these events, the people you meet and connect with can tell their colleagues in other companies about your work and expertise if you make a good impression and nurture the relationship after the event. No matter the event type or place, you have to make an effort to actually talk to people you don't already know. The success rate of in-person contact is much higher than waiting to be found online. Meetup.com, Eventbrite.com and even Facebook have a lot of events and meetings you can attend for free or for a minimal fee.

Luisa Zhou, entrepreneur and writer for GrowthLab, made $1.1m in eleven months through online communities. Zhou wrote in a post, 'I started spending all my free time hanging out where my potential clients were online (free Facebook groups) and directly engaging with them by sharing valuable content and answering any questions I could about advertising. That's how I got my first client' (Zhou, 2017). Zhou was awarded a $5,000 contract by a woman she helped to set up an advertising campaign. She gave free advice initially and was asked to work on a related project. You can use similar strategies to win your first clients. Help someone in an online forum, answer a question on Quora, or comment in a subreddit community.

Network with other freelancers

Starting and building relationships with other independent workers in related industries is one of the best ways to get client referrals. Use this approach to your advantage.

Find meetup groups, online communities, social networks groups and make meaningful connections. Events and meetups are great places that offer amazing opportunities to build a long-term relationship with other on-demand workers. Other freelancers are not your competition; working alongside them, rather than against them will benefit your career in the long term. You can find and use shared office locations where independent workers meet. Make yourself useful and don't aim to just benefit from them. Be of value, earn their trust and they are likely to recommend your services to their past or current clients.

Team up with another independent contractor

If finding clients in the beginning is challenging for you, try partnering with an established freelancer or agency as a subcontractor. This can help you offer even better services to attract bigger projects. When they get a big, new project or just have more work than they can handle themselves, they'll call on you to help out. It can turn into repeat work, referrals, and ongoing contracts that brings you consistent income. You can also team up with another consultant that provides a complementary service and develop a unique service for your clients. For example, a writer and an SEO consultant could team up to deliver an all-in-one package for businesses. This way, you're both getting work, you're utilizing two people's networks, and the client gets an amazing finished product. It's win–win. In general, teaming up makes it possible to deliver greater guarantees and to tackle larger projects.

To explore this route to find work, decide what you want to focus on, identify the opportunities you want to work on, and find suitable freelancers you can work with. Use the on-demand platforms we discuss in Chapter 10 to search for skilled workers in your industry or other markets that can complement your skill. Building a network of freelancers can give you an opportunity to scale your work beyond your immediate capability. However, with every partnership comes potential risks. Be realistic about expectations. Don't go into partnerships without stating clearly your responsibilities, and how much each party will stand to benefit from the team effort.

Connect and follow influencers

Influencers in your industry have authority. They command respect and trust. People and businesses take their advice and business seriously. Find relevant ones on Twitter, LinkedIn, Facebook or Instagram. Once you have identified those in your niche, mention them, retweet them, share their work with your followers, like them and mark them as favourites. You can even ask a couple of them to write for your blog when you launch. Ask one or two to mentor you. Keep them updated (without being intrusive) on how you are progressing. They can become advocates for your work. This could possibly be your home run! It takes time to build relationships with influencers. Be patient. You may not get response for a very long time but don't stop reaching out and asking for help.

Leveraging personal passion projects

Working with clients is great, especially when you get to that point where you are consistently working on projects every month without missing out on regular income. But working on your own successful projects changes your perception of independent work. You will have the rare opportunity to make extra recurring income, and create something awesome for your portfolio. And, most importantly, you will stay interested in and motivated in what you do every day. You can start a new project by solving your own problem. What frustrates you? Think about something you use on daily basis that can be improved. Or a product you use that can be changed or made better.

Postanly, my weekly newsletter that goes out to over 45,000 people every week, started as a personal project to find the best articles to read. It's a free email digest of the best posts about behaviour change from around the web. I had been using Pocket (an app for managing a reading list of articles from the Internet) to save articles to read later but wanted a way to share my list with other people who follow me, so I created Postanly Today. Postanly Weekly is a profitable newsletter that generates income through sponsorships.

If you're a writer, you can write a book. A designer can launch and sell amazing designs online. Tools like Shopify and Etsy can help you sell your designs. If you engage well with people, you can start a podcast (an audio show, usually spread across a series of episodes) about a topic you deeply care about and interview influencers in your industry. You can become a coach to help people solve problems in your niche or turn your expertise into a coaching business and sell coaching packages to individuals or businesses. Bear in mind that whatever you choose to do will help you build up your reputation and in the long run it will allow you to get more clients.

Finding the extra time to launch a personal project can be super-tough especially if you have a lot on your plate. But if you schedule time for it, and choose to work on an idea you are passionate about, you will be motivated enough to make time for it. Don't work on a project you don't deeply care about. Self-initiative is not easy for most people, but think about the long-term impact of your own creation. Even if it fails, you would have learned something new, improved yourself and be better than everyone else who isn't trying to achieve their dreams.

Key takeaways

- Thriving as an independent worker is about positioning. And it's also about communicating the right message to potential clients.

- To improve your chances of success, focus on pitching how you intend to solve problems for your clients. Is your message about what you do clear enough? Your target clients should understand your specialty when they land on your website.

- Take and unconventional approach to attracting clients. Offer a solution to a problem your prospective client faces for free, and in return ask for referrals, testimonials or future business. Or, better still, answer questions for free on niche groups to win their business.

- Leverage relevant online platforms and show you work in the best way possible.

- Make the most of offline niche events. The success rate of in-person contact, is much higher than waiting to be found.

- Self-initiative has enormous benefits. Create your own projects to put you in the best position to work with big brands. You can bring more purpose and joy into your life in the process. You will have the rare opportunity to make extra recurring income, and create something awesome for your portfolio.

- Working with clients is great, especially when you get to that point where you are consistently working on projects every month without missing out on regular income. But working on your own successful projects changes your perception of independent work and brings you fulfilment.

References

Goins, J (2017) One of the oldest lies many people believe keeps too many of them from earning money, 22/6 [Online] uk.businessinsider.com/why-you-shouldnt-work-for-free-2017-6?r=US&IR=T

Robinson, R (2016) Six-figure freelancers share their best advice for finding success and clients, 20/4 [Online] www.forbes.com/sites/ryanrobinson/2016/04/20/six-figure-freelancers-share-their-best-advice-for-finding-success-and-clients/#3b3865f6119e

Zhou, L (2017) Exactly how I made $1.1m in sales in 11 months, 9/2017 [Online] growthlab.com/how-i-made-one-million-luisa-zhou

05
Saying no to freelance work

A huge part of doing business as a gig worker is finding paying clients. Declining work may not be the ideal thing to do, but in many cases it makes a lot of sense. Working on the wrong project, or accepting to do work that will not advance your career, can do more harm than good. In this chapter we will explore why it's important to turn down some clients, and discuss how to choose projects that align with your skills, values and long-term goals. We will also learn about setting priority filters to help you choose better projects, and build relationships with both potential and repeat clients. We will end the chapter with email scripts you can use to decline offers of work.

The power of a positive no

As a freelancer, it pays to get used to saying no, especially when you manage your own time. It is acceptable to say no, irrespective of what is being asked and who is asking. Overcommitting yourself will disrupt your ability to focus. You can't have time both to commit to anything as well as delivering results if you say yes indiscriminately to every request that comes your way. It's impossible to make time for work, family, friends and even yourself if you can't turn down some of the many requests you receive. You need to take time for yourself and focus on the most important things to you in life without feeling any sense of guilt or obligation.

Many freelancers say yes to almost every gig, even if they are not in line with their strengths. They get comfortable saying yes and this is to their own detriment. They don't have the courage to say no when it's necessary and important for their careers. Most gig workers will accept any project that comes their way because they worry their luck will run out if they turn down projects. They are concerned that they will never find more gigs. People who are at the beginning of establishing a career are more likely to say yes to almost everything because of the fear of missing out on opportunities. But saying no is necessary to build a profitable freelance career that you actually enjoy. Many freelancers turn down a gig or project for many reasons, including: low compensation; short timeframe; ethically or morally questionable request; asked to take on more work when you're already busy; you don't like working for that particular customer; or the work doesn't advance your freelancer career. Does this sound like you?

The hard part is communicating your response to the prospective client. Learning to say no is necessary to build a profitable and fulfilling freelance career that you will actually enjoy. 'No' is an option you should get used to. It's liberating and helps you to focus. In their book *How to Say No Without Feeling Guilty* (2001), Patti Breitman and Connie Hatch observed:

> Out of guilt or fear of confrontation, we take on more projects, invest in someone else's priorities.... In the process, we dissipate our most valuable personal resources – time, energy, and money – on things that aren't important to us. Each time we agree to something without enthusiasm for interest, we waste a little more of these precious resources.

You must remember that saying no is not self-serving, rude or contemptuous. Saying no allows you to work on projects that bring out the best in you and allows you to grow. It helps prospective clients find someone who will give their task or project the time and attention it rightly deserves. It's difficult to turn down work, but saying no means saying yes to something else that requires your full attention. As you get experience, build your portfolio and become good at what you do, you will have to learn how to allocate your time and focus on the right projects.

How you disengage with clients is the key. Paulo Coelho, author of *The Alchemist*, said, 'When you say "yes" to others, make sure you're not saying "no" to yourself' (Coelho, 2006). Declining an offer can actually be a positive step. If you hate disappointing clients, saying no can be very hard for you. If you don't say no, it would mean that you will agree to work you feel you should do, instead of saying yes to projects you really want to do. Don't put your independent freelancer career into jeopardy.

You lose your sense of control if you keep saying yes to every project. Beyond money, you should take on gigs to build your reputation and a lasting career. Find work that inspires and build a great portfolio for your long-term future.

Say no for a better yes

Independent work can take up a greater percentage of your time, even when you really don't want to work. The race to meet deadlines on the many projects and tasks on your plate can be overwhelming, especially if you are a popular on-demand worker. As a gig worker, you are probably juggling many deadlines on a weekly basis.

Say no to projects that will most likely waste your time. When you choose to work for yourself, you are responsible for your total well-being. It's your job to put your own needs first. To make your freelancer career sustainable, it's important to learn how to say no to clients and make tough decisions that will protect your interests in the long term. It pays to set boundaries. Having a strict policy on projects you take on means you can be more open to other, better opportunities and earn more. With better projects in your portfolio, on top of a fulfilled freelancer career, you'll be able to provide much more value to your clients.

Should you turn down work when you're too busy? For good clients, try not to. If you are totally booked for a couple for weeks or months, find an alternative worker or supplier for them. For one-time clients you're not likely to work with again, you can turn them down if their work is not a good fit. If a good and steady client wants you to work on a high-profile assignment or emergency task, try to fit them into your schedule. In some cases, an outright 'no' as a response may not be necessary. If the client isn't in a hurry you can communicate your ideal completion time for approval. For example, you can send this response if you are not ready to take on the project or assignment yet: 'I can't work on the project at the moment, but I am available on [insert date and time].' Always remember that a project delayed/denied is much better than a project derailed.

The importance of a priority filter

Prioritization can be really difficult for a gig worker. To succeed as a freelancer, you need to be really tough with yourself and be selective about tasks and projects. You are the only manager of your time, work, money and long-term future.

Every freelancer needs a work structure or framework. It's the best way to choose and work on projects without wasting time. You always need an idea of what it will take to finish any gig you accept. Planning applies to both your time and money. As an independent worker, time is your most valuable limited resource. Invest it like a valuable asset. It's important to know exactly what you need to do at any point in time. A priority filter can help make a decision about short-term tasks, gigs and long-term projects you should take on.

These questions can help you decide whether to say yes or no to work:

- Do you have time to take on the tasks at this time of the month?
- How much is the gig paying and is it worth your time?
- Is the project or task a good potential recurring business?
- Will the project help advance your career?
- Will this client's name look impressive in your portfolio?
- Does the work excite you?
- Will it advance your long-term career goals?

If you keep accepting and saying yes to contracts that don't fit with the above, you are probably wasting your time on the wrong projects. If you can't answer these questions positively, don't take it on unless you're really struggling to pay the bills. Any time you take on a gig that's just okay, you could be missing an opportunity to take on a project that could make a lot of difference for your career. Empowering yourself to say no will give you the time you need to focus. Think about the kind of work you want to be doing in the long term. For many freelancers, it could be a minimum fee. Others work with small businesses within a certain industry. Whatever it is, think about the type of projects you want to showcase in your portfolio and where you want to be as an independent contractor in one, five or ten years from now. If you have standards and guidelines, you will not be seeking every gig to make money.

Stephen Covey, author of *The 7 Habits of Highly Effective People*, argues, 'You have to decide what your priorities are and have the courage – pleasantly, smilingly, non-apologetically – to say "no" to other things. And the way to do that is by having a bigger "yes" burning inside' (Covey, 2004). Learn to identify your goals, prioritize them and work on meaningful projects that bring out the best in you. Be clear on your values and work ethics. When you know what you want in your life and career, what to do, and when to do them, it becomes easier to say no. Don't get stuck in a project you definitely don't want.

Hold your boundaries

Remember, you're your best and in many ways your only advocate. You know your skills, your strengths, and your passions and vulnerabilities. You know what you expect from your freelance career. Now, you just need to know when something is worth your time. If it's not, don't hesitate to say no. And when you do, be professional, respectful and gracious about it. Communicate your response to the request to your client or potential client and let them know that the project isn't right for you or that you aren't right for the project.

Knowing when, how and why you need to say no

We've just seen why it's important to say no, but knowing how to tell a potential client no is just as important as knowing the why. As many of the responses you will use to decline assignments will be similar, save time by writing and saving email scripts you can personalize for clients. If a project is not the right fit for you, turn down the client immediately without delay. Keeping a client waiting and eventually telling them you can't work on a task can end badly for your reputation. Be straightforward and give the actual reason why you can't work on their project at this time. Sometimes, the concern you have will be addressed by the client, meaning that you can proceed. People will appreciate your candour and will trust that you will be a good partner due to your willingness to openly communicate. Even if you don't accept to work on the project, you'll have established your brand and reputation. That may lead to referrals, and it will also help you feel good about your choices.

Make the client feel you still value the business relationship, even though you can't work on the current project. Reassure them of your interest in working with them in the future. If they can wait, offer other dates in the future when you will be available, or recommend other competent on-demand workers (make sure you notify anyone you recommend, give them details of the client and the project in question). You can also encourage would-be clients to check in with you again at a particular date. This frees them up to find another on-demand worker for the job, but ensures that you are still open for other gigs in the future. Don't close doors entirely on a good client.

How to say no without hurting your client relationships

Building relationships with clients improves repeat business and increase your chances of getting referred. Competition for clients is fierce when you work for yourself. Saying no is empowering, but it's tough. It's therefore imperative that you turn down gigs in the best way possible.

Email scripts are the best way turn down clients without wasting too much time thinking about your response. You will also make it easy for potential clients to contact you again in the future. These are a few scripts you can use to turn down work nicely.

Example one

Hello Sam,

Thank you for getting in touch. This project sounds amazing.

Unfortunately, I have a tight schedule at the moment [or: I am not in the best position to accept new clients].

However, if you need assistances with similar projects or tasks in the future, I will be happy to help.

Best regards,

[Your name]

Example two

Hi Rebecca,

Thank you for your email.

I appreciate the opportunity to work on your project.

Regrettably, I am not taking on new projects at this time of the year. If that changes, I will of course let you know immediately.

However, I'd like to recommend the following companies/people/resources that should be able to help you out.

Don't hesitate to reach out in the future.

Thank you,

[Your name]

Example three

Hello Sophie,

Thank you for thinking of me for this project and taking the time to contact me.

Sadly, my calendar is full for the next six months. But I can connect you to a few contractors who are capable of delivering equally great work. Please check out their portfolios at _____ and _____.

Hope that helps.

Best,

[Your name]

Example four

Hello Joe,

Thank you for reaching out, but I'm currently tied up with _____ at this time. However, I'd be more than happy to forward your details to one or two other potential on-demand workers.

If you ever need help with other tasks in the future, you can always feel free to contact me via email or give me a call.

Regards,

[Your name]

Example five

Hi Chloe,

Thanks for your email.

Your project is an amazing challenge, but the scope falls out of my skills set.

It's ideal for _____ [link to one of your contacts who can take on the project].

I can forward the project description to them, if that's okay with you. Alternatively, you can take it from here and reach out to them.

Thanks again.

[Your name]

These scripts are the basic structures you will need. You can modify them for different clients.

Here is a summary of the process for turning down a project:

- In your opening reply, show your appreciation.

- Be expressive about your yes. In a paragraph or two explain your reason for declining the gig and why now is a bad time.

- Propose a yes. Offer a different schedule if that will work for them. Recommend another gig worker or friend who can deliver equally good work. You can even direct them to resources they will find useful to help with their project. Create a win–win situation if you can, especially if you want to work with them in the future.

Key takeaways

- While you can't always avoid saying no, what you can do is build the best positive no. Learning to say no is necessary to build a profitable and fulfilling freelance career that you can actually truly enjoy.

- You have every right to turn down and gracefully reject projects that fall outside your core competence, or that do not bring out the best in you.

- Saying no means saying yes to something else that requires your full attention.

- Prioritization can be really difficult for freelancers. To succeed as a worker, you need to be really tough with yourself and be selective about tasks and projects. You are the only manager of your time, work, money and long-term future.

- Saying no sets boundaries that can help you evaluate whether a project fits your business path and life values.

- Learn to identify your goals, prioritize them and work on meaningful projects that bring out the best in you.

- As many of the responses you will use to decline assignments will be similar, save time by writing and saving email scripts you can personalize for clients.

References

Breitman, P and Hatch, C (2001) *How to Say No Without Feeling Guilty: And say yes to more time, and what matters most to you*, Broadway Books, New York

Coelho, P (2006) *The Alchemist*, Harper Collins, New York

Covey, S (2004) *The 7 Habits of Highly Effective People: Powerful lessons in personal change*, Free Press, New York

06
Getting real work done and staying productive

Working for yourself means you have multiple jobs, with several clients who require deliverables at different times. When you work like that, you need priorities, work ethics, ways of working and procedures. That makes time management a bit tricky, since every day – or even every hour of the day – might not be the same as the last. This chapter focuses on the key principles for staying productive. We will discuss ideas for creating a working schedule, how to build a productive routine, how to deal with distractions and how to find your flow.

Managing yourself

Finding focus is becoming the biggest challenge for independent workers. When no one is checking you're on target or exceeding expectations, and you only have yourself to answer to, it can be hard to reach your goals or meet client deadlines. We've already discussed that working for yourself can be fulfilling, but with that freedom also lies a number of pitfalls. You can easily find yourself adrift without the structure of an office setting, and lose concentration because of the flexible hours, freedom and the seemingly endless amount of 'free' time that gig workers seem to enjoy.

Managing yourself can be hard if you don't have a work ethic. It's hard to carve out hours of productive time when you are constantly distracted and overwhelmed by information you don't need. As an independent worker, your career depends on your ability to single task, meet deadlines and deliver on your promise. Hence the more productive you can be, the more work you can do, and the more you can ultimately earn.

Your time is money

Time is your most valuable resource when you choose to work for yourself. Keeping a strict control over how you manage your time is critical, otherwise important things get neglected in favour of urgent things. In some cases, you realize you forgot to send invoices (again) and that really exciting proposal is overdue, and the project you're working on is slipping on its timeline. If you juggle multiple projects at the same time, the value of prioritization cannot be overemphasized. Time, as it turns out, can work in your favour or against you. Planning and maximizing your time translates to better profitability. It can also create extra space in your personal life to do other personal things.

Scheduling work

The most effective people in life have systems, routines and schedules that guide their actions and choices. Your ability to work according to a timetable can make all the difference if you want to be successful. Effective freelancers thrive on routines. You can avoid burnout, sleepless nights and missed deadlines if you have a working routine.

Jessica Greenwalt, a freelance graphic designer, voted 2012's top freelance designer by DMZ Interactive, advises on being productive, 'The productivity trick I've used that has made the biggest impact on my life is using lists. I've been using Google Calendar as my daily checklist. I fill up to eight hours of each work day on my

Google Calendar with tasks, blocking off a minimum of 30 minutes for each one' (Kraus, 2015). Personal structure allows you to work orderly and better without missing deadlines. Think of your tasks in categories called the 'three Cs': creative, collaborative and connecting, says Kevin Kruse, author of *15 Secrets Successful People Know About Time Management* (Kruse, 2015).

Categories make it easy to find and work on tasks without wasting time. This prevents mixing team or collaborative work with personal projects on the same list of things to do.

Set realistic timelines

Every project you accept will be different. Requirements will vary. Time to complete every one of them will not be the same. Your past projects can serve as a guide for making projections about future projects. If you are working on multiple projects, plan your timelines to make sure you don't compromise any of them and miss deadlines. You can work faster by breaking big projects into phases or milestones.

Building a productive routine

Effort alone can't help you stay productive. If you can manage both your time and effort, you can easily work smarter and faster, and build skills like focusing and concentration in the process. Your approach to work has everything to do with your productivity level. If you spend time optimizing your working practices, strategizing your routines, planning for future work, you will achieve your short-term and long-term goals. Jocelyn K. Glei, host of the Hurry Slowly podcast, was quoted as saying, 'Kicking off the day without a plan opens you up to the dangers of "reactive work," letting other people's demands dictate what you do with your day' (Vozza, 2016). Start your day with an action plan, and know how you want the day to end. That way, you won't have react to every request you have not made plans for in the day.

Define your own 'office hours'

You need to set a time you begin working and a time to quit at the end of the day. You can't work when you feel like it and stop at odd hours. You will burn out. Plan work hours around your day and be disciplined about how you work. Keep Parkinson's law in mind when you start working on a new project or task. Parkinson's law states that 'work expands so as to fill the time available for its completion'. To avoid falling victim to Parkinson's law, set yourself personal deadlines ahead of your actual client deadlines and aim to finish the work ahead of schedule. This will give you enough time to make revisions if necessary or work on something else that could bring in more income.

Start your day on purpose

Start your day in the right way, and you will use your time and energy on the right tasks at the right time. Stephen Altrogge, a writer at Zapier, explains, 'Morning and evening routines prime you for success. They help you achieve more, think clearly, and do work that actually matters. They keep you from thoughtlessly stumbling through your day and make sure you get the most important things done' (Altrogge, 2017).

Create a checklist for your daily tasks

If you planned what you're going to do today, yesterday, your time will be put to great use and you will accomplish your goals and milestones. You will spend your day acting and getting things done, instead of reacting to what others expect of you at the wrong time. Plan your day the night before. Make a list of everything you want to accomplish and how long it will take to get them done. You work better when you can visualize tasks and know exactly what needs to be done on any given day.

Checklists keeps you from forgetting important short-term jobs you need to do for your clients. They make it easy to work on projects without thinking about what to do next because you have a visual representation of what needs to be done. Good checklists are precise, says Atul Gawande, author of *The Checklist Manifesto*. He writes:

> They are efficient, to the point, and easy to use even in the most difficult situations. They do not try to spell out everything – a checklist cannot fly a plane. Instead, they provide reminders of only the most critical and important steps – the ones that even the highly skilled professional using them could miss. Good checklists are, above all, practical.
>
> (Gawande, 2009)

A work checklist frees your mind to concentrate on to focus on high-level thinking and important tasks.

Create both weekly and daily task lists. Use your weekly task list to capture all things that need to get done during the week. As with the daily list that you create the night before, your weekly list should be created before the week begins, ideally on Sunday night or before you end any given week. Use your daily list to write down immediate tasks for the current day. Maintaining two lists can help you visualize high-level projects and associated tasks for all ongoing projects.

Use the Pomodoro technique

You've probably heard of this approach to work. It's an effective way to work in sprints, avoid distraction and focus on tasks one at a time. Francesco Cirillo developed this time management technique in the late 1980s. The Pomodoro approach to work uses a timer to break tasks into, at most, 30 minutes sprints, with a break of about five minutes between each task. You work for a period of time without distractions, rest for five or ten minutes, repeat the process for four sessions or more, and then take longer breaks. There are Pomodoro apps for both Android and iOS devices. You can also use the timer on your smartphone.

Once you commit to using the Pomodoro technique for your work, turn off notifications and block off distractions because if you have a tendency to be distracted by emails, notifications, or other interruptions you may have some difficulties using this technique.

Break every project into tasks you can manage

When you work on big projects with a structured approach for tackling tasks, you can easily get distracted. Small tasks that are part of a bigger project can be completed faster

John Reeve, web designer, developer and co-founder at Pelago, explains, 'The idea is to break down each project into tasks that correlate to client deliverables. This way, each task can be closed out as its deliverable is completed' (Reeve, 2014). For all your daunting projects, separate milestones into simple do-able tasks. For any big project, take a few minutes to think how long it will take you and all the actionable tasks you need to do to complete it. It can get you started quicker and will help you complete it as planned. You can use the Pomodoro technique for this strategy of work.

Mange your energy

You are more active and can work better in the mornings. The first two to three hours after you wake up are your peak times for getting a lot of work done. 'Our body temperatures start to rise just before we wake up in the morning and continue to increase through midday,' Steve Kay, a professor of molecular and computational biology at the University of Southern California, told the *Wall Street Journal*. This gradual increase in body temperature means that our working memory, alertness and concentration also gradually improve, peaking at about mid-morning (Dovey, 2016).

The end of the day is therefore the worst time to do your most important and creative tasks. Your daily energy, willpower and ability to focus depletes with time on any given day, so focus on doing your best work before lunchtime. You are likely to be caught up in a vicious cycle of procrastination if you tend to push your work to late afternoons.

Make time for personal development

Your growth as a gig worker is as important as projects you work on for your clients. Make time in your schedule for networking, personal growth reading, and life improvement courses and podcasts, as well as time to reflect on what is working and what is not working. Reading or listening to self-improvement content on Fridays is a great way to end your week. Investing in yourself should be a priority to help you work better and improve your approach to personal and business goals.

Schedule breaks on purpose

As a gig worker, you can easily lose control your time. Don't take breaks for granted. They are important for your total well-being. Always write down 'breaks' on your to-do list. It pays to take an interest in activities unrelated to work, as this can be a way to recover from active work. Stimulating leisure activities outside your everyday tasks and interests can avoid burnout and offer a greater ability to overcome challenges in what you do for a living. Find something to do outside work. It's not a stretch to predict that your extracurricular activities outside work can make your workday hassles easier to handle, relieving some of the self-induced pressure and opening up some creative energy that can be directed at impending tasks.

Make plans to spend even your breaks purposefully. You could use them to check your emails, go for a walk, check social media updates or meditate. Break times can also be used to reflect on goals, tasks and projects. The novelist and social critic Charles Dickens wrote between the hours of 9 am and 2 pm. After that, he would go out for a long walk.

> IF I COULDN'T WALK FAR AND FAST, I SHOULD JUST EXPLODE AND PERISH
> **CHARLES DICKENS**

Robert McCrum wrote about Dickens' work habits in the *Guardian* and said, 'you discover that Dickens, in his prime, used to compress his literary energies into five hours... after which he would walk incessantly, and put his mind into neutral. He might return to what he'd written in the morning later in the evening, but those five hours held the key to his output' (McCrum, 2011).

Take time to pause within yourself momentarily every now and then to re-fuel, re-new and reflect. Think, take control and measure your progress. You need downtime to refresh your brain. The only way to prevent yourself from being burnt out is to take an intentional break. Mental breaks allow your brain to distance itself from work for a short period of time. A refreshed brain can focus better and engage more deeply when you start work again.

Dealing with distractions

Distractions are perhaps the biggest enemy of productive work. All the emails and notifications you receive daily can steal precious time you need to concentrate on productive work. They may not be a big deal in the grand scheme of things, but when combined, all that time could be used effectively to advance your goals. Freelancers don't have all the time in the world for everything. It's a myth. Set your priorities right and make that clear to your loved ones, friends and clients to improve how you work. When you work for yourself, people tend to think that because you're not working in a nine to five setting, you're accessible at all times.

Distractions can vary from a single, urgent but not important email to multiple phone notifications. They kill productivity. Distractions are anything that interrupt your focus. There are many online and offline distractions that may be stealing your concentration and ability to do focused work. It's not easy managing time and holding down distractions when you maintain flexible working hours. Strict work rules, motivation to get work done and self-control can help you finish off all of your tasks with little or no outside distraction. Without a set of rules that guide how you work, you're giving the flexibility of your schedule permission to interrupt with completing daily tasks.

Until you shut down the doors to distractions, the road to a successful freelancer career will be a long one. Use batch processing to respond to anything that needs your attention that is not work. If you can't automate tasks and concentrate on your work, you could check emails, reply to messages, share social updates or browse your social feeds at a certain time of the day.

> YOU WILL NEVER REACH YOUR DESTINATION IF YOU STOP AND THROW STONES AT EVERY DOG THAT BARKS
> **WINSTON CHURCHILL**

According to a report by the McKinsey Global Institute, people spend an average of 13 hours per week, or 28 per cent of an entire working week, on emails (McKinsey Global Institute, 2012). Instead of reacting to each notification, turn them off and check them at 11 am and 4 pm every day. That way, you won't have to answer every message you receive. Consider turning off notifications for apps on your phone – you shouldn't be checking them every time a new one comes in. You can never get real work done on time if you keep reacting to every 'snooze' from your phone.

Track how you spend your time

How are you currently managing your time? You can't improve what you don't measure. Distractions come in many forms. Sometimes, it isn't just Facebook or YouTube videos, but it's work itself. Measure your progress every week to find out if you are actually getting things done. Time tracking apps like RescueTime, Toggl, Hours, Timely and TopTracker can automatically track how you spend your time. You can start measuring how you spend your time to help you figure out everything that's distracting you every day. The more projects you work on at a time, the more necessary it becomes to maintain a detailed and specific schedule each week, hence the need to know how you are spending your time. Knowing your productivity drains can help you create a strategy to overcome them. Take back control of your time and you can do more and better every week.

Finding your work flow

In the end, independent work management is very personal. No two freelancing schedules are the same. There are many productivity methods, procedures, systems and techniques you can use. A productivity system enables you to manage and execute your commitments, and get real work done with little or no distraction. A few popular productivity systems include Getting Things Done by David Allen, Personal Kanban Approach to Work, and the Eisenhower Matrix. The goal is to try a few and settle on a system that works best for you. Experiment with different routines, work hours and schedules, and repeat those ones that brings you the most results. As an independent worker, there are no productivity rules you need to follow, but there are standards and systems that have been proven to work well. Use and stick to the ones that brings out the best in you.

Key takeaways

- Time management is an important element of making it as a freelancer.

- If you can manage your time and effort, you can easily work smarter, faster and build skills like focusing and concentration in the process.

- Set yourself personal deadlines ahead of your actual client deadlines and aim to finish the work ahead of schedule to give yourself enough time to make revisions if necessary.

- Use the Pomodoro approach to work in short intervals with breaks in between tasks. Break projects into small, achievable tasks to complete them faster.

- The road to a successful freelancer caree will be a long one if you can't manage distractions.

- No two freelancing schedules are the same. Experiment, measure and stick to the productivity system that works best for you.

References

Altrogge, S (2017) 12 morning and evening routines that will set up each day for success, 14/2 [Online] zapier.com/blog/daily-routines

Dovey, D (2016) When does the brain work best? The peak times and ages for learning, 8/8 [Online] www.medicaldaily.com/when-does-brain-work-best-peak-times-and-ages-learning-394153

Gawande, A (2009) *The Checklist Manifesto: How to get things right* [Online] www.goodreads.com/work/quotes/6862414

Kraus J (2015) What freelancer schedules actually look like, 23/05 [Online] www.sitepoint.com/freelancer-schedules

Kruse, K (2015) *15 Secrets Successful People Know About Time Management: The productivity habits of 7 billionaires, 13 Olympic athletes, 29 straight-A students, and 239 entrepreneurs*, The Kruse Group, Philadelphia

McCrum, R (2011) The best of times to write, 27/10 [Online] www.theguardian.com/books/booksblog/2011/oct/27/best-times-to-write

McKinsey Global Institute (2012) The social economy: Unlocking value and productivity through social technologies, 12/7 [Online] www.mckinsey.com/industries/high-tech/our-insights/the-social-economy

Reeve, J (2014) Three ways to break down a project into manageable tasks, 22/09 [Online] www.myintervals.com/blog/2014/09/22/three-ways-to-break-down-a-project-into-manageable-tasks

Vozza, S (2016) 8 productivity experts reveal the secret benefits of their morning routines, 11/03 [Online] www.fastcompany.com/3065263/8-productivity-experts-share-their-morning-routines

07
Managing your finances

Cash flow is king in the gig economy. Keeping your finances organized can keep you in business for as long as you want. As a gig worker, you are responsible for managing your invoices, paying your taxes and minimize your expenses while maximizing your working hours. When you work for yourself, staying fiscally prudent is as important as delivering on your deadlines. In this chapter we will focus on managing your personal finances and how to get paid on time. We will look at personal budgeting, savings, managing taxes, how to invest and, finally, discuss planning for your financial future.

Savings

As a freelancer, your finances can be daunting but they're also a vital part of your life. Even though we all know that we should be saving, few people do. It's even more important for gig workers. Make saving a priority. Alongside an emergency fund, you should be saving regularly into an account that works for you. Saving for the immediate future is only part of a healthy savings plan. By taking control of your money and implementing good financial plans, you can find both stability and freedom as a freelancer.

Save twice as much for emergencies

The importance of an emergency fund for freelancers cannot be overemphasized. Incomes will vary every month, and long- and short-term gigs will bring in different incomes. Your ability to manage and save as much as you can is key to your success.

Don't underestimate how big your emergency fund should be, because as a business of one (discussed in Chapter 3), a lot depends on your ability consistently to show up and work on your projects. Regular income is not guaranteed. If you decide to take time off to go on vacation, or a medical emergency pulls you away from your work, you will rely heavily on your savings. The basic financial advice for freelancers is to always save enough money to cover at least six months of your monthly bills and expenses. An even better approach to your finances is to save more than you will need for at least a year, if you can. The benefits of savings are enormous. You will be able to choose your clients carefully and work on projects you deeply care about. You can choose to work only on projects that advance your career. You'll feel more comfortable saying no to gigs that are not a good fit for you. And you can deal with delayed payments without stressing out. You can also take advantage of more opportunities to network, upgrade your skills or spend time with your family without worrying too much about putting off clients.

Personal budgeting

One of the most important money principles in life is to spend less than you earn – whether you are an independent contractor or a full-time employee. Knowing where your money comes from and where it goes is the key to better budgeting. Budgeting can be daunting, especially if you make money from multiple sources, but with better planning you will have everything under control.

Use separate accounts for business and personal transactions

As your one person business grows and you begin to receive payments from multiple clients and engage the services of subcontractors to manage tasks like editing or graphic design, things can get complicated. When you clients increase and business is growing, managing money becomes more complex. Separating your business and personal accounts can simplify your budgeting processes. Business accounts should be strictly used for client payments and paying business-related expenses. Your rent, mortgage, utilities and shopping expenses should be paid from your personal accounts.

Your life will be a lot easier, especially when it comes to taxes, if you separate your business from your personal finances.

Pay yourself a 'salary'

To ensure your personal finances are kept separate from your business, pay yourself from your business account. Use your average income for a certain time period (the past 6 or 12 months) to calculate how much you need to pay yourself every month, then automate your other expenses. As your income will fluctuate every now and then, it's important to reassess your financial situation and make adjustments where necessary. During months when your income is higher than average, you can still pay yourself the same amount to compensate for months when income is lower.

The first step is to figure out your monthly income. Remember, you should take into account other business expenses including taxes, health insurance and retirement pension (all of which can be deducted from your business account) before you settle on the amount you want to pay yourself.

Track your income

Knowing how much you bring in each month helps you plan better. It's important to have a historical view of your income over a period of time to be able to prepare for both busy and slow times of the year. The proactive method is to track who paid you what, when and how much. If you have records from the last six months, or year, determine your average from that.

Know what you're spending

If you don't already, start tracking your spending. You can do this in whatever way you are most likely to stick with – a spreadsheet, a notebook specifically for managing your finances or one of the numerous financial apps that aim to help you manage your money (we will discuss a few good options you can use later in this chapter). If you don't know much you spend every month, try to come up with an average figure.

If you use a financial app, it should be easy to see your average monthly figure. If you don't, add your monthly necessary recurring expenses – housing, transportation, utilities, groceries, education, debts, savings, retirement, taxes (talk to a tax professional about how much tax you need to pay, preferably someone who specializes in self-employment) – and then, using your log of expenses or bank statements, come up with an average monthly figure for your spending.

Seeing what you spend in an organized way gives you the ability to see patterns in how you spend. Once you know how much is going out every month, you are better able to make financial allocations and spend prudently in the future.

The 50/20/30 rule for budgeting

Establishing good financial habits will last a lifetime. The 50/20/30 budgeting rule can help you make better future financial plans. You don't even have to make a lot of money to use the rule. This useful method can help you spend your money responsibly. It's a simple way to divide your after tax monthly income into needs, savings and wants. Elizabeth Warren, a Harvard bankruptcy expert, popularized the 50/20/30 budget rule in a book she wrote with her daughter Amelia Warren Tyagi, *All Your Worth: The ultimate lifetime money plan*. The rule puts 50 per cent of your income toward essentials, like housing and bills, the next 20 per cent of your budget towards long-term savings and extra payments on any debt you may have, and finally the last 30 per cent towards wants or personal spending, like dining or entertainment. Having just three simple categories lets you stay focused on your budget and goals as you move towards better financial stability in your career as an independent consultant. So how does this break down, and how can you apply it?

50 per cent of your income goes to essentials

Essentials are things you need to get by day to day. Payments for housing, food, utility bills and transport are essentials. They are expenses you have to pay no matter how much money you earn. Everyone has almost the same types of expenses.

No matter what you make, your total spending in this category should not be more than 50 per cent of your net income. The trick is to adjust the cost of individual items and spend prudently. For example, if you live in a high-rent city, housing cost will be high compared to other items in this category. But for those in low-rent cities, rent may be low, and they may spend more on other individual items in this category. The sum is more important than the individual costs. The percentage is the maximum you can spend.

Spend 20 per cent on savings

The next step is to dedicate 20 per cent of your income after tax and monthly essentials to your financial priorities, to create a comfortable level of funds to avoid taking on future debt. These include things such as savings accounts, investments, retirement plans, emergency funds and paying off your debt. Making arrangements for this category may not make sense especially when you have other needs to take care of, but it will certainly become more pressing in decades to come. The most important thing to keep in mind is that when you start saving early, you will earn compound interest over time, especially if you take advantage of long-term investment opportunities.

Use 30 per cent for personal spending

Expenses that enhance your lifestyle fall into this category. Anything you spend money on for your personal enjoyment can be classified as a personal expense. Things like monthly entertainment, personal travels, holidays, gym memberships and other extracurricular activities qualify as personal spending. They are everything you buy that you want but don't necessarily need. You decide which expenses are wants and needs. But remember, you can only spend 30 per cent on personal expenses, according to the 50/20/30 rule. If you can plan to spend less in this category, you can have more money to invest towards your future.

The 50/20/30 budgeting rule is a recommendation. Everyone's financial circumstances are different. It's a framework you can use as a guide. Your income and expenses will determine what's best for you. You can only create a budget based on your unique situation. If the 50/20/30 rule won't work for your present financial circumstance, create a financial plan that allows you to limit you expenses, save and invest prudently in your future.

Create a system for managing your money

How do you track and manage your invoices and expenses? Make life easier for yourself by creating a system for managing your money. A financial system is a way to automate the day-to-day money decisions you have to make as a gig worker – creating and sending invoices, paying bills, investing, cutting down on spending, increasing spending on things you love and focusing on the things you care about. Automating your finances can help you get more things done with less effort, and it will also help you minimize errors.

Put your finances on autopilot

It pays to automate as many of your financial transactions as possible. Automating your finances involves making arrangements to take care of your financial tasks and obligations so they require little management. When you put your finances on autopilot, you put financial structures in place to take care of your bills, taxes, investment and budget without spending time each month going over your finances. Automation can help free up your time so you can focus more on the work you enjoy. When you choose to automate, it's still important to periodically check in on your monthly payments to make sure you haven't miscalculated, or overpaid your bills.

Automate your bills

If you haven't already, create a bills folder in your email account and move all your weekly or monthly payments to it. This will make it easy to know what to put on autopilot. Take advantage of direct debit to automatically pay your monthly bills. You can start today by listing your recurring monthly bills, and then opening another bank account with online access, just for your recurring fixed monthly expenses. Many banks allow you to manage your money via an app. Set up automatic payments so that your recurring monthly bills are now paid out of your new 'bill pay' account. This account should be used to cover less flexible expenses, such as mortgage or rent, electricity, insurance or debts you need to pay.

Automate your savings

It's important to make plans for future and life's surprises. That's why, in addition to your income and bill pay accounts, you should open a third account just for saving. Set up a direct deposit from your income account to this third account but make sure it has no check writing, bill pay, or debit card features. Use the 50/20/30 rule we discussed and transfer 20 per cent of your income after tax to your savings account. This money should be hard, though not impossible, to access.

Put your investments on autopilot

Many freelancers feel they don't have the extra money to invest. In most cases, however, there are some ways to save a bit extra. Your investment goals will determine how much of your savings should go into an investment account. Make a list, estimate the amount you'll need out of your savings account for investment purposes, and contribute a specific amount to your investment portfolio every month. You can choose from a variety of stocks, bonds, funds, etc (we will discuss your options and the tools you can use in the 'Investment' section below).

There are often other tax breaks available when it comes to saving and investing. In the UK, for example, an Individual Savings Account (ISA), a tax-free way to save or invest, allows residents to save up to £20,000 (2017/18 tax year) a year completely tax-free. Tax breaks are country-specific. Research any tax-advantaged accounts and investment opportunities you can access.

Managing taxes

Tax law is ever-changing. A common dilemma for many self-employers is knowing how much they are going to owe in estimated taxes. If you don't have an accountant yet and have no idea how much to set aside, start with 30 per cent of your income. Set aside a percentage of every payment you receive. This saves you from having to guess how much you think you might earn over the course of the year. And it will be easier to pay that as taxes as you plan your budget. It takes discipline to save in advance for the tax year; after all, you have other expenses to take care of. But it is equally important to pay income tax. You can make things easier for yourself by setting up a savings account just for your taxes. You can then link that account to your business account and automatically transfer 30 per cent of your income when you get paid.

Keep track of your receipts

Noting down your expenses and keeping receipts are essential for tax purposes. It's so easy to lose track of all the little items you buy to keep you in business. For tax purposes, it's important to create or use a system that will help you keep track of all your expenses. This means you'll have to keep hold of receipts, invoices and bank statements. One increasingly popular way of managing finances and expenses is through online apps. Many expense tracking apps allow you to connect and view bank feeds, manage transactions, send invoices and upload details of your expenses.

Expenses are easier to maintain when you use a single platform to view, track and manage them. These apps simplify your paperwork. They are also handy for tax returns. Many financial apps for freelancers, such as FreeAgent, can help you track your income and expenses, and even make it easier to file your taxes without missing a deadline. Expensify is a robust app for both small businesses and freelancers who have expenses scattered across paper receipts and online transactions. FreshBooks, another great invoicing app, allows you to send invoices, track time, and manage receipts and expenses.

Planning for your financial future

As a freelancer, you are really no different from anyone else when it comes to retirement. If you intend to work as an independent contractor for a very long time, it's important to start planning your future today. Ghilarducci, author of the book *How to Retire with Enough Money*, says freelancers should plan on retiring at the age of 65. 'Even if they want to work longer, there is no guarantee that anyone will want to pay them past this age,' he says (Rafter, 2016). Plan for the next 20 or 30 years, or even more, without working, when you think about retirement. If you're in your twenties or thirties, retirement is a long way away, and probably doesn't seem like a priority. But retirement is really expensive. If you don't start early, you simply won't have time to build up 20 or 30 years of money you need to live a good, full life. And in that time you may have health problems or need constant care. It's important to plan for your financial future without hesitation.

A survey by the Small Business Majority found that four out of ten freelancers don't have an active retirement plan (Small Business Majority, 2017). It's so easy to put off thinking about retirement when you work for yourself, but it's important to aim to set aside a portion of your monthly budget towards retirement. 'If you want to have enough money for retirement, aim to save at least 10 per cent of your salary every year if you are in your 30s, 15 per cent in your 40s and about 40 per cent in your 50s,' says Dan Rafter, Money Rates Columnist (Rafter, 2016). Planning and saving for retirement can a big challenge for any freelancer contractor, but it's a necessary step to a better and financially stable future.

Pension investment alternatives

Plan for a deeper pool of investment options when you choose to invest your savings for a better return, especially if you have an unstable income. It can help cover emergencies in the future and provide the safety net you need during lean times. Whether you're the sole director of a limited company or an independent contractor, making regular payments into a self-employed pension is also a great way to reduce your tax bill. With an emergency fund, stick to a safe, instant-access bank account, because it's money you need to access when necessary without delay. But when you're saving for longer-term goals, you can afford to take more calculated risks to boost your returns. When you choose to invest your retirement funds, think diversification. Use general funds instead of single stocks. And don't hesitate to invest in other parts of the world. Combine both short -and long-term investment options.

Make the most of tax-free investment accounts

In the UK, options include a personal pension, and a self-invested personal pension (SIPP). If you are self-employed you can also join NEST (National Employment Savings Trust), an 'auto-enrolment', government-backed scheme. It is designed for the workplace but also accepts independent workers. It's a good idea to spread your money across a combination of a pension plans. ISAs products, including the Cash ISA, the Stocks and Shares ISA and Lifetime ISA are also available to on-demand workers. An ISA allows you to save up to £20,000 a year completely tax-free.

While self-employers in the US don't have access to 401(k) plans (a retirement savings plan sponsored by an employer), you can still set up and save in a Simplified Employee Pension (SEP) Individual Retirement Account (IRA), especially designed for freelancers. Many financial institutions provide this service. They also allow self-employers to save on a larger scale. According to Beth Kobliner, a financial journalist and author of *Get a Financial Life: Personal finance in your twenties and thirties*, 'There are two types of IRAs, Roth IRAs (which offer completely tax-free growth) and deductible traditional IRAs (which offer an up-front tax break and then years of tax-deferred growth)' (Kobliner, 2018). Other investments US self-employed residents can explore include the Savings Incentive Match Plan for Employees (SIMPLE) IRA and Simplified Employee Pension (SEP) IRA.

Retirement plans and products are country-specific. Find out what works best in your country and start planning for retirement today, not tomorrow, next month or next year.

Key takeaways

- As an independent worker, your finances can be daunting but they're also a vital part of your life. Make savings a priority. Alongside an emergency fund, you should be saving regularly into an account that works for you.

- Use the 50/20/30 budgeting rule. The rule puts 50 per cent of your income towards essentials, like housing and bills, the next 20 per cent of your budget towards long-term savings and extra payments on any debt you may have, and finally the last 30 per cent towards wants or personal spending, like dining or entertainment.

- Put your finances on autopilot. When you put your finances on autopilot, daily, weekly or monthly budgeting decisions you have to make – paying bills, investing, paying taxes, increasing spending on things you love – are taken care of whilst you focus on getting real work done to make money.

References

Kobliner, B (2018) Yes, freelancers, you can save for retirement, too! [Online] bethkobliner.com/advice_basics/freelancers-savings-retirement-ira

Rafter, D (2016) Guide to saving for retirement when you're self-employed or freelance [Online] www.money-rates.com/personal-finance/save-retirement-self-employed-freelance.html

Small Business Majority (2017) Freelancers need flexible retirement options [Online] www.smallbusinessmajority.org/our-research/workforce/freelancers-need-flexible-retirement-options

08
Building a pipeline of work

Finding clients and marketing yourself to your target audience are the biggest struggles for many freelancers. While the tasks can seem daunting, with the right plan, approach and resources, they don't have to take all your time. The good news is that finding work is easier today than it used to be. Independent work sites are bridging the gap between businesses and on-demand workers. That means you can have a healthy, flowing pipeline of work. In this chapter we will look at how to build a pipeline of work for consistent gigs. We will discuss prospecting, promoting your work and how to take advantage of networking. We will explain the best approach for responding to ads on gig job boards, how and where to advertise yourself for work, what to do when you are looking for work from current and past clients, how to leverage meetings, conferences and online social platforms for work.

Prospecting

If you can learn how to find great clients, and then get a greater percentage to consistently offer you gigs, as an independent worker everything else will be easy. Prospecting can be hard for new gig workers, especially since there is no single approach that works for everyone. It's different for everyone, which is part of what makes it both difficult and valuable. However, you are basically just trying to find people who need what you're selling and then you have conversations with them about the work that you do. Easier said than done, I know. Prospecting works if you make it a part of your schedule. People really do want to pay you for what you do. It takes time and effort, but done right it can help grow your independent work. We will be sharing exactly what you need to do to get gig work, and all the resources you need to make the process easier for you.

Focus on high-probability prospects

Prospecting is contacting the right people and businesses with the sole intention of securing work. You find people who you think you might want to work with, contact them, and follow up until you get a response or don't think it's worth your time anymore. When you prospect, you don't just sell your services to strangers, you also introduce yourself to the right people and businesses that could be clients in the future. Prospecting is effective when you define your target market, narrow your search and focus on prospective clients who have the greatest need for your service.

Customize your message

Don't send the same prospecting message to different people; tailor them to individual clients. And send them to the right people to get the best results. One way to send a personalized message to your prospective clients is to find out information about them before you before you call or email. Start the process on their website – read team pages and press releases, and gather as much data as possible. Read about new projects they are pursuing, find out who handles marketing, prospecting, partnerships by reading the 'team' or 'about us' page. It's a way of finding a reason to make contact, and make your emails effective and relevant. When you're prospecting – making calls, sending cold emails, connecting via social media, pitching at conferences – your focus is on building relationships with those who may want to do business with you, now or in the future.

Get introduced

One of the best ways to reach out to people you want to work with is to reach out to them through people you and they already know. Use LinkedIn if the prospect you want to reach is connected to your contact. LinkedIn has a function on their mobile app that will set up an introduction for you. If you can say something like, 'Your contact, Richard Lawrence, suggested I give you a call...', your chances of success go up ten-fold.

If you need one of your connections on LinkedIn to introduce you to someone or a business, you can use or modify the email script below.

Hello [name]

I hope you've had a good day so far.

I noticed you [refer to their recent career move, their status update about work or a project they are working on].

How is it going?

I'm reaching out because I want to pitch my _____ services to _____. According to LinkedIn, you know [mention the connection] who works for_____.

Do you mind connecting us via email? Your endorsement would make a lot of difference for me.

Thank you for your help. I really appreciate it.

Best,

[Your name]

Create a system for building a client pipeline

Reaching out to potential clients is an ongoing process for gig workers. When you're really busy with work, things like reaching out to potential clients can often be left off your list of things to do.

It's important to set up a system for building a sustainable client pipeline that can guarantee some amount of work every month. The easiest way to secure the best gigs is to create a solid process for yourself that ensures you find high-quality work in a timely manner.

The five-step system for prospecting

Prospecting takes time and effort. If you invest time into finding new clients, eventually you will get a recurring income from many of your clients who have ongoing projects. Creating a system for organized pitching is the key to getting clients.

Step one: Create a general picture of what your ideal client looks like

Define your target clients and narrow your pitches to high-probability people and businesses. Don't spread yourself too thin. You will spare yourself a lot of time pitching to businesses who either can't afford your services or don't need what you offer. It also allows you to go out and identify businesses that fit the description. Create a spreadsheet for profiling. Gather information for each business on the industry, revenue, location, number of years in existence, funding status, contact person/email. Use your spreadsheet to keep track of potential prospects, when they were contacted, what response you got and those you have to follow-up.

Step two: Automate your searches

Start your search online to create a list of leads and input them into a spreadsheet. Instead of manually searching relevant sites every day for leads, set up an email system that delivers results to you via email. You can use IFTTT (a free automated online service that connects services, websites and other sources with each other) for this.

Step three: Set up a schedule for reaching out to prospects

Once you automate your searches, schedule a time for reaching out to them. Reaching out for gigs can also take up a huge part of your week. Even if you have a consistent schedule, a busy week can keep you from your regular reach-out schedule; but you will regret it when the busy time is over and you are floundering for clients. An important part of working for yourself is making time for the 'business activities', prospecting being a huge part of these!

Pick a certain day of the week to find new clients, or plan to send out a number of emails before a certain time of the day. For example, on your calendar you can write specific goals like 'I will devote Thursday mornings to finding new leads', or 'I will send out five prospecting emails before midday every Tuesday'. The key is to make it a habit and stick to a consistent schedule. When you pitch or find new leads at the same time every week, you will avoid the interruption that comes with prospecting, and make time to get work done without distractions.

Step four: Find and use templates

You will be pitching your services to a number of potential clients every week. Save yourself some time and speed up your work by creating an email script or template you can customize for prospective clients. You can save your template in Evernote (a note-taking app) or create a canned response in your email.

Here is a sample script you can use and modify, depending on the service you provide.

Subject: Regarding Your _____ Ad

Hi [name]!

I found your job advertisement on [name of the website] about _____ (answer specific questions in the posting, if any).

I've worked with popular brands over the past ___ years, including _____(provide links to their sites). You can check out some of my previous work on my portfolio at [link to your portfolio]. I have a few ideas on the best way to approach your work.

If you're interested, I'd be happy to send them to you. We can also discuss them via phone or Skype.

If you have any question about my work, please don't hesitate to let me know.

[Your name]

It's simple, doesn't sound like a spammer, and arouses the client's curiosity to reply back.

Step five: Keep pitching

Don't stop pitching when you land a few clients. If your calendar is full for a period of time, you can focus on your deliverables; otherwise, it's important to consistently pitch for new clients. If you get retainer clients (agreeing to regular commitments or long-term work) in the process, you won't have to pitch every week.

The different ways to land gigs

Clients are the lifeblood of any independent consulting business. Without them, you can't pay your bills and you certainly won't survive as a gig worker.

Job boards

You may already use job boards. They are effective and businesses consistently post projects and assignments on them. A gig board is one of the easiest ways to find work. There are lots of options for different industries, and they cover contract work, part-time jobs, and even long-term projects. Gigster, Crew, We Work Remotely, Krop, Reddit For Hire, AngelList, Upwork, Y Combinator Jobs, Product Hunt, Toptal, Guru, 99designs, Freelancer, Peopleperhour and Indeed are a few of the popular options you can use. There are many others, but these fifteen can help you get the right kind of gigs. Some of the sites require you to sign up and create a profile. Other may ask you to prove yourself through tests that showcase your skills. Whatever skill or service you offer, these gig platforms will help you find work.

Ask for referrals

For every gig you successfully deliver, don't hesitate to ask for a referral. Referrals can get you more clients, faster. Ask your best, happiest and most favourite clients for referrals. Happy clients will gladly spread your name to other businesses or colleagues if you ask them for a referral. Many clients are sometimes busy and won't go out of their way to recommend your services. Take the initiative and ask for a referral if you did great work.

To get the best referrals, give specifics of what types of clients and work you are looking for so your clients can help you find work to fit your skill. You can modify the email sample below to help you get referrals.

Hi [name]

I'm delighted you are satisfied with the work.

I'd appreciate it if you can pass my name along to businesses in your network, colleagues or anyone who would be interested in what I do.

Can you recommend any company that could use my services right now?

Thank you

[Your name]

Keep the email short. Be concise about exactly what you want. And don't leave it open-ended. The email should necessitate a response, otherwise they may not take action.

Partner with agencies

There are many agencies out there that work with big brands. And sometimes if the brand has a low budget, or agencies have no interest in the project, they pass the assignment on to a gig worker. Some agencies don't have the required skills to work on the task, hence the need to work with experts like you. It's another great way to work with new clients. When you reach out to relevant agencies, email the person in charge of building relationships or partnerships, or better still the person who can make the decision to work with you. Here is a sample email you can use to reach out to agencies in your niche.

Subject: Working Together

Hello [name]

I am a huge fan of the work you do at _____. I really love [products or services you like on their website]

I work with a lot of startups/high-growth companies. Past clients include _____. A complete list of my clients can be found here _____.

I wanted to reach out quickly to see if you need [your skills] for any overflow of work for some of your clients.

I am available for a chat this week.

Regard,

[Your name]

Reach out to old clients

Chances are, you have dozens of contacts you have been in touch with either within the past couple of months or was close to working with but due to schedules couldn't accept or take on the project. These are people you can follow up about possible work. They may not have projects or assignments for you at the time of reaching out but they will keep you in mind for future projects. It's the best way to remind old clients that you are looking for work.

Promotion

Promotion involves both online and offline activities that show your services to the right audience. When done right, it can improve how you attract clients.

Leverage testimonials

If you sell your services online, testimonials can boost your promotion efforts. It's a proof that the services you sell works. Testimonials add credibility to your promotion efforts, make it easier for prospective clients to hire you, and show the quality of your work through satisfied clients.

For every successful work delivered, ask for testimonials you can publish on your website. Many happy clients are willing to help you succeed as an expert in your field, and won't mind connecting their name to your work. When you ask for testimonials, make it easy for your old clients to commit to writing you the preferred endorsement that can help you land new clients. The emails you send should be short, considerate and easy to reply to, whether they respond with a no or a yes. Example:

Hello [name],

I've really enjoyed working with you on _____ project. Would you be willing to give me a testimonial quote I can use on my website?

I will link back to your website to help with SEO for your website.

I can draft a quote for you and send it to you for approval or I can send you a couple of questions. Let me know what's easier for you.

Thank you

[Your name]

The perfect testimonial details the problem your ideal client had and how your service or idea solved their problem, and provides evidence of accomplishments or results.

A testimonial framework can help you get a response faster. For every email, you send to ask for an endorsement, ask the client if they are comfortable to use it a simple script. Alternatively, you can provide a few questions for them to answer. For example:

1 What problem did I solve for you or your business?

2 How has your work or project improved since I delivered on the task?

3 If you were to recommend my services to other businesses, what would you say?

Put your best testimonials on the homepage of your website, or on your popular pages.

Capture leads

Leverage your personal website to capture emails of potential clients. Apart from your contact form, an email subscription form is one of the best ways attract prospective clients. SumoMe is a popular lead generation tool you can use to capture emails. Emails can help you build relationships with people who visit your website. Many people don't give away emails easily on websites. You can overcome that obstacle by giving away an educative eBook, a free consultation when they sign up, or by promising to solve a problem in your industry, in exchange for their emails. You can contact them later and ask about problems in their businesses you can help solve.

Run ads

Google Adwords can help you advertise your services to the right audience. LinkedIn and Twitter also run ads you can use to target specific clients. Microsoft's Bing Network is another ads option similar to Google Adwords. You can easily set a small daily budget on one or two of the ad platforms to try it out and then do more of what works for you. You'll drive traffic to your site and can try to develop that traffic into leads. Both Google Adwords and Bing Network have a steeper learning curve than Facebook, LinkedIn or Twitter. They take a while to set up and take time to pay off. You can learn how to run effective paid campaigns at PPC University, an educative resource put together by the pay per click (PPC) experts at WordStream, a paid search software company.

To improve your ad conversion rate, run targeted ads that have a specific value proposition, give away something of value (informative eBook works best) in order to get them on your mailing list, and then continue to provide value (lead nurturing) until they decide that they trust you enough to reach out.

Share educational content

Blogging, creating eBooks, and sharing informational products about topics that tie into your services are amazing ways to build relationships and become an expert consultant. They can also get you introduced to some amazing people. Brands can reach out to you directly to hire you to do work for them through your informational products they find online.

Networking

Traditional networking is still the best way to acquire new clients. Online and offline networking is one of the most active ways to get gigs. For new gig workers, it can be an uncomfortable and awkward part of getting new clients, especially if you are an introvert. But it can be a rewarding experience, so think of the time and money spent at these events as an investment in yourself and an opportunity to make real contacts with prospective clients, and with a bit of practice you may actually have a little fun in the process!

Use both offline and online networking opportunities to reach out to prospective clients. LinkedIn remains one of the best social tools for online networking. Complete your LinkedIn profile with up-to-date information about yourself and your work. To get the best results from LinkedIn, import your contacts, and connect with many people. Keep your status updates current by sharing relevant content with your connections. Take advantage of LinkedIn groups, answer questions related to your niche, offer to solve problems and you'll not only grow your connections, but you might also get paid work from some of your connections.

Don't restrict yourself to professional contacts; make sure your friends and family know what you do. They can refer your services to their professional network. You can also use social media to reach out to people who may need your services. Like any business relationship that takes time to grow and build trust, you have to consistently build and maintain great relationships as you grow. Your success will largely depend on the business relationships you nurture.

Thought leadership

This is one of the best ways to attract prospective clients. But it takes hard work, discipline and consistent work to be recognized as a thought leader in your field or niche. Thought leaders have built their brands and reputations over time. Writing and speaking are the best strategies for becoming a thought leader. You probably can't start reaching large audiences tomorrow, and its pretty difficult work compared with sending responses to emails. But establishing yourself as a thought leader in your space can attract influential brands.

Ideas to get started

You can't be an influencer from day one, but you can purposefully build your career in that direction. You can start by teaching what you know at a small Meetup, launch a free online course to educate your clients, or publish your content on sites like Quora and Medium. You can also start an educational series over the course of a month on how to accomplish a specific task in your niche. Guest post on popular industry blogs. Start a podcast (an episodic series of digital audio or video files that a user can download and listen to), host webinars (an online seminar that turns a presentation into a real-time conversation from anywhere in the world), reach out to smaller blogs and podcasts in your niche and ask about being interviewed about your craft. You don't have to try all of them at the same time – just think of a few ideas you can consistently do every week. See what kind of reaction you get. Measure the results and focus on what works.

Key takeaways

- When you start prospecting – making calls, sending cold emails, connecting via social media, pitching at events, etc – your focus should be on building relationships with those who may want to do business with you, now or in the future.

- One of the best ways to reach out to people you want to work with is through people you already know.

- Creating a system for organized pitching is the key to getting clients. The easiest way to secure the best gigs is to create a solid process for securing work that ensures you find high-quality work in a timely manner.

- Use relevant gig boards for finding work. A gig board is one of the easiest ways to find work.

- For every gig you successfully deliver, ask for a referral. It's one of the best ways to get clients faster.

- Use testimonials to your advantage. Endorsements are proof that you can deliver on your promises. They add trust to your marketing efforts.

- Sharing free informational products (eBooks, case studies, infographics, blog posts) about topics that tie into your services is an amazing way to build relationships and become an expert consultant.

- Traditional networking remains one of the best ways to get new clients. Make time and plan to go to an industry event or a conference to connect with industry leaders and influencers.

09
Managing
your clients

Clients sustain businesses, and they are indispensable to the self-employed. Every business or person you choose to work with is potentially a returning client, so make sure they have an amazing experience working with you. Your clients will have different goals and expectations, so you need to invest in building and maintaining a strong relationship in order to build trust and credibility. Good client relationships will help you get paid on time, get excited about work every day, and thrive in business. A bad relationship can often lead to frustrations, late payments, and misunderstanding. In this chapter we will look at how to build and maintain client relationships, set up a successful system to manage your clients, the best ways to communicate with your clients and useful tools for client relationship management.

Building and nurturing relationships

Winning clients is a difficult process so you need to nurture and hold on to the right clients. Business is essentially about people, understanding how to work with them and maintaining strong relationships with those people who are your best customers. Better client relationship management is about treating people with respect and being honest about what is humanly possible. Be authentic about what you can do within the timeframe, and be open about how long it takes to get the work done. Don't lie to win a contract;

you will not perform well when you over-promise and under-deliver. In addition, the long-term implication of misleading a client to win a project can be bad for your reputation. When your client requests task updates or asks about deliverables, a professional approach requires that you act with respect and take a genuine interest in the person as well as the project. Be ambitious, challenge yourself but be mindful of your strengths and weaknesses.

Set up a communication system

Defining your communication channels right from the beginning of your gig career can save you a lot of time, simplify conversations with different clients and help you work on different projects without difficulty. Your choice of tools is dependent on how your client wants to communicate with you in the course of the project. Whether you choose to use email, Slack, Skype, a collaboration tool or a combination of these, stick to the same ones for each customer. This is especially important when your clients request revisions, feedback or consistent updates. You can discuss your preferred methods of communication at the start of each project and explain why, how and at what stage of the project you will use each channel. This makes it easy for them to prepare, sign up and set up different channels to make the process easier. If your deliverables are a combination of text, audio and video, it pays to make it clear to your client how you intend to submit results.

Create boundaries

When you're in the gig economy, you run the risk of doing everything, even outside work hours, in fear of missing out on future work from the same clients. If you are hoping for a testimonial, the urge to work extra-hard gets stronger. Boundaries can help you stick to basic rules no matter the incentive or motivation. Boundaries give you the freedom to work without unexpected requests that steal your time and energy. They allow you to focus on your work and serve your clients better. Don't be afraid to make known to your client what is, and what isn't, acceptable. If working on a weekend is not an option, be sure to communicate that to your clients. If you don't answer calls and emails outside office hours, make that known to them. Enforce these hours, even if you work from home or with a laptop at a coffee shop or a co-working space. The idea is to plan your breaks so that you avoid working around the clock and burn out. You can easily set up an auto-email reply during 'off-hours' to tell your clients how soon you will get back to them, or what they can do in the meantime if their communication is urgent.

Start every project with a contract

The expectations of every job or task should be in writing. Decide on the terms of each project alongside your client; both of you should discuss and decide the working terms. A contract eliminates uncertainty, so write a simple agreement for your clients to make sure everyone is clear on what needs to be done. It should specify deliverables, timelines and scope of work and payment, resources you will use to get the work done and what you expect your client to pay. Fees, extra work rates, late fees, and when you expect payment should be included. Be very specific about your payment terms and conditions. How do you invoice your clients? How do you expect payment to be made? How long do they have to make part or full payment? What is your refunds policy? To avoid payment issues, request a deposit before you begin. In many industries, an upfront payment of 30–50 per cent of your estimated fee is acceptable. Don't agree to payment terms that involve payment only upon the complete delivery of work. You don't want to work on a project for months only to have the client reject it and pay you less than you deserve.

Do you expect them to pay for additional resources? For, example, should they pay for subscriptions to services you don't use? If so, make that clear. If they have to provide stock images or certain materials to get the work done, write that in the contract before the project starts. A concise and clear contract offers the security you need to focus on your work knowing that you have both agreed to the same terms. You can re-use your contract template for different clients in the future. PandaDoc can help you create your contracts in easy steps. You can also edit their standard contract templates for your needs. If you send your contracts via email, you can use RightSignature to sign your documents.

When in doubt, ask more questions

Don't make conclusions and assumptions about what your client wants. Many freelancers are shocked by their client's feedback when they submit their initial draft, deliverable, or first completed assignment. The only way to avoid the first draft disaster is to ask lots of questions about what the client wants. As the expert, your first task is to understand their problems before you come up with a solution. When you get inside your client's head and start speaking their language, you will avoid a lot of unnecessary or redundant work. Double-check the details to get clarity on anything that might be unclear, confirm the facts first and then get to work. For every problem, clients have a desirable outcome in mind. Project descriptions sometimes don't specifically communicate client expectations.

Get a calendar

Mapping your tasks and activities for the day or week is a powerful way to design your life. A calendar shows you all the important and time-sensitive must-do actions at a specific time. You can use your favourite calendar app to block out time for personal activities including time with family, exercise and breaks from work. Scheduling your tasks on a calendar instead of writing them on a to-do list can help you work better, and will reduce the stress of knowing when to work on a task and deliver it. When you use a calendar app, label crucial dates or, better still, create a system for your due dates: some tasks can be labelled 'important' and others 'urgent'.

Important things on a calendar include specific tasks that help you complete projects. Urgent tasks are things you need to respond to immediately, like calls and emails. This can help you focus and work on tasks that need your immediate attention before making time for others. If you create project-specific calendars, invite your clients to share these. Google Calendar is a free and useful app you can use for all your needs. Clear, Sunsama and Wunderlist are great Google Calendar alternatives. If you have a lot of projects with different timelines, you will need a robust project management tool instead of relying on just a calendar.

How to get feedback

Feedback is crucial to your success as an independent worker, even more so if you expect your clients to refer your work to other businesses and colleagues. An honest review of your deliverables can help you improve on what doesn't work and do more of what works. If you want clients to engage your services in the future, seek genuine feedback from them when you complete assignments. Address every issue that could potentially be a future problem, or any obstacle as the project progresses, instead of waiting for feedback at the end of the contract. You can build periodic reviews or progress review meetings into your personal timeline. A good practice is to schedule short meetings with your clients when you are 30 per cent into the project and also when the project is 70 per cent complete. Make it brief, listen instead of talking about what you have done, and ask open-ended questions. Examples of these include: 'What do you think about…?' or 'What do you want me to change or develop?' Your focus should be on gathering information to improve your final deliverable. After every feedback session, send the client a summary of what was discussed, and actions you will take to show that you have taken the feedback on board and that you intend to implement the recommendations. You could even go a step further by sending the client a list of the changes you will be making in the next few weeks.

The goal of a scheduled feedback meeting is to ensure that you are working according to a plan and addressing concerns the client may have with how you work, as well as any doubts they may have about your deliverables. Steve King, a Partner at Emergent Research and a writer for the Harvard Business Review, explains, 'Set yourself up for positive feedback by ensuring that you and your client are in agreement on the project plan and deliverables right from the start. Problems that come up are often due to a lack of clarity on that assignment's goals, schedules and/or deliverables' (King, 2015). If you don't understand anything about an assignment, communicate your concerns, be clear about expectations and work with the client to deliver exactly what is expected of you.

Take criticism as a feedback

One hundred per cent client satisfaction is a dream for every business or consultant. Unfortunately, not everything goes as planned or expected when you provide a service. In the course of your career, some clients may not like your final delivery, how you work or communicate, or may even want you to restart the project or tasks all over again. However critical their feedback, remember you're running a business, so don't get personal about it. In all situations, maintain a positive attitude in your response to your clients, be open to recommendations and suggestions, and don't take feedback, or rejection of your work, as blanket judgments on you as a professional. If the criticism is vague, ask specific questions to dig deeper and find out what the real issue is. This will help you find a solution to their concerns.

If you keep getting the same criticism from multiple clients, you will have to take time to reflect on your particular style of work or your behaviour and open yourself to learning and changing how you work.

Criticism is an opportunity to learn more about yourself, and about the client, and a great chance to convert them from being merely satisfied to a happy client who could offer repeat business in the future. In all feedback situations, take a step back, and review how you can improve how you work. In some situations, it's probably something you missed because of a tight schedule or deadline: use criticisms to your advantage. If all efforts to turn an unhappy client into a satisfied one proves futile, politely explain to your client why the relationship cannot be saved and move on with both your and your client's reputation intact.

Handle delayed payments professionally

Payment delays are one of the biggest challenges every freelancer faces. Over 70 per cent of freelancers have trouble getting paid at some point in their careers, according to research by the Freelancers Union, the non-profit group that promotes the interests of independent workers (Knight, 2017). Payment problems can impact your business growth and how you work. When your finances suffer because of late payments, you can't focus and concentrate on getting work done. When handled wrongly, payment issues can ruin a great client relationship.

An invoicing app can set gentle reminders at scheduled intervals to keep your relationship with your clients in great shape while still ensuring their prompt payment of fees. If no one is responsive to your reminders, escalate to a phone call and speak to the right person, preferably someone in the accounting department if you are working with a reputable company. If you work with popular brands or companies that use payment cycles, you need to find out and understand when and how they make payments. In many situations, you can overcome the payment cycle problem by establishing your own frequent billing cycle that works for you, and make that clear in your contract. For longer projects that require weekly or monthly deliverables, ask for milestone payments. These improve cash flow and ensure consistency for both you and the client.

How to fix a broken relationship

Like any business relationship, things can always go wrong. Many freelancers cut ties with clients too soon. Your willingness to work things out with a good client shows your professionalism. In all situations where a relationship is at stake, seek to find the cause of the problem. Did you make a mistake? Did the client expect something different? Was it an issue of miscommunication? When you know what the issue is, you can take steps to fix it. If you made a slipup, take the blame, suggest a solution, be open to ideas, feedback and change, where necessary. In many situations, a broken relationship can be fixed, but in some cases it's better to move on. Even if you can sense a relationship is coming to an end, don't burn bridges. You never know how or when that person or client might come back into your life.

Client management tools

If managing multiple projects becomes a challenge, you will find a project management tool very useful. It gets you out of your inbox, creates a single platform for managing your documents, files and tasks. More importantly, a project management tool will create a timeline for your entire project. Once you get used to your best tool, you will find other benefits and options to make your life even more easier to manage. You can plan your projects before you begin them, assign tasks to others if you tend to hire or collaborate with other freelancers, organize resources, predict future challenges and even identify problems before they arise. The right tool puts you in control of your client's projects, eliminates chaos and enhances your work life. Asana, Trello, Freedcamp and Basecamp are a few of the best tools you can use to manage your projects when you are dealing with a long list of clients.

One of the best features of these tools is that repeated activities like weekly updates or progress reports can be automated. They can help you reduce the time you spend sending emails about your progress. You can easily use both Asana and Trello to notify your clients automatically about updates when you check off tasks or move them to 'in progress or done' columns. To streamline communication with multiple clients, invite them to your trusted tools, shared Cloud folders you have created for projects, and other ways you share data, documents and project information.

Key takeaways

- Good relationships can earn you referrals, repeat business and testimonials for future work.

- Defining your communication channels right from the beginning of your gig work career can save you a lot of time, simplify communication with different clients and help you work on different projects without struggle.

- Don't agree to work on any project without a formal agreement that lays out the scope of the project, timelines and the payment terms, and ensures that expectations are clear for you and the client.

- Once you sign the contract and begin to work on a project, provide support at every step of the way, and make it easy for them to understand and work with you right from the beginning to the end.

- When in doubt about project descriptions, don't assume what the client wants – ask questions, do your homework first and get all the information you need before you begin a task or project.

- To streamline communication with multiple clients, invite them to your trusted productivity or project management tools, shared Cloud folders you have created for projects, and use other ways to share data, documents and project information.

References

King, S (2015) How to get feedback as a freelancer, 19/09 [Online] hbr. org/2015/08/how-to-get-feedback-as-a-freelancer

Knight, R (2017) How freelancers can make sure they get paid on time, 15/09 [Online] hbr.org/2017/08/how-freelancers-can-make-sure-they-get-paid-on-time

10
Leveraging online platforms for gig work

The increased accessibility of technology platforms means businesses can tap into an even bigger list of global independent contractors. The self-employed once heavily relied on their business cards and networking events to promote themselves and pitch their services. Work was limited to how many people and businesses they could reach. Influenced but not limited to technology, independent work is undergoing a major transformation. This chapter explores and explains the many ways technology is helping gig workers find work and the best ways that freelancers can leverage technology to promote their work and expertise.

Choosing the right online platform

Online talent platforms are changing the way people and gigs are matched, creating efficiency in hiring and improving productivity for businesses. Today, with just a laptop, a relevant skill and the right online site, on-demand consultants can find work across the world. Experts in many industries, including writers, developers, marketers, analysts and researchers are marketing their services on different online portals, landing gigs and making money in a more efficient way than ever before. As technology improves and new options emerge, more and more people will have better opportunities to sell their services online, no matter their location. Choosing the right online site to sell yourself or show your past work will become even more important.

Digital platforms for finding work

Flexible work platforms have reduced the time people take looking for gigs, saving freelancers a lot of time and improving their chances of finding work faster. There are thousands of freelance websites and apps for many industries. If you are completely new to freelancing, these sites are the best places you can start registering for gigs. Experienced freelancers know many of the sites listed here. To make the most of out of a general freelance site, focus on pitching a specific skill you are good at instead of listing everything you can do.

Upwork

Upwork used to be two separate freelance work sites: Elance and oDesk. After a merger, both sites were rebranded as Upwork. It's one of the largest freelancing sites online and offers skilled work to almost every skill level. To succeed at Upwork, you have to complete your profile (with sample of past work and references) when you sign up and build up great reviews, experience and amazing customer relationship. You can pay to upgrade, which opens up a lot of gig opportunities for you.

TaskRabbit

Anyone who does home repair and improvement will find TaskRabbit very useful. The app matches self-employed people to local demand. The tasks on the platform are mainly low-skill categories including moving goods, cleaning, delivery cleaning, mounting and installing electronic devices, flat-pack assembly, heavy lifting and general handy work in a house.

Fiverr

Fiverr is a robust marketplace for digital services including design, marketing, writing, translation, video creation, audio, advertising and programming. The platform used to have a $5 base price for all gig work but the company has changed its business model and currently allows gig workers to set their base prices.

FlexJobs

If you are looking for hand-screened flexible, freelance remote, and part-time jobs, register at FlexJobs. The site connects flexible workers with popular brands like SAP, Apple, Hilton, Xerox, Dell, Salesforce and PwC. FlexJobs can even find you full-time remote work. Job seekers pay a membership fee to get full access to the site and discounts on remote working productivity tools.

Toptal

Toptal provides highly skilled on-demand workers for startups, medium-sized businesses and big brands like J.P. Morgan, Hewlett Packard, Zendesk and Pfizer. The company recruits only the top 3 per cent of independent consultants through a rigorous application process. Successful applicants have proven track record and rich industry experience in business, technology or design. Toptal experts include thousands of people in over 100 countries.

Amazon Flex

If you have a car and don't mind driving for Uber or Lyft (both ride-sharing apps) or making food deliveries for Deliveroo (available in selected cities in Europe and Asia), you can check out Amazon Flex. Amazon's flexible work option allows you deliver items and earn money based on the number of deliveries made. Amazon runs a background check when you join the programme and asks you to watch instructional videos on the app.

99designs

99designs is one of the largest on-demand design marketplaces. It's open to skilled designers globally. Designers submit quotes on projects and clients choose the designer they want to work with based on fee, experience, reviews and sample past work. Freelancers can also participate in a design contest submitted by clients. Popular projects include logo, web and app design, art and illustration, packaging, book and magazine design, and general marketing and sales design projects.

Guru

Freelancers and clients connect and collaborate on Guru to work on short-term projects. You can create a Guru account in minutes, browse jobs, submit a quote and begin the process of getting hired for a project. Clients pay by the hour, milestone, task or by using recurring payments. The site offers a daily job-matching feature to notify freelancers of good opportunities that match their skills.

Freelancer

Freelancer is one of the largest independent consultant digital marketplaces. Clients hire experts in job categories such as software development, sales and marketing, accounting, legal services and engineering. On-demand workers bid on relevant projects and clients choose to work with freelancers they find suitable for their jobs. Alternatively, clients can direct offers to freelancers they find suitable for their work.

Contently

Contently runs a digital marketplace for freelancer writers, and designers, and editors. It matches Fortune 500 companies to skilled content (text, image, video, audio) creators. The site allows you to create a portfolio page on the freelance section. You can use it to promote your work and get more gigs. To succeed on Contently, build a strong collection of past work that can attract higher-paying gigs. The company reaches out to freelancers when they find a match for their skills and background.

PeoplePerHour

Clients can hire skilled experts in hundreds of different categories of work on the PeoplePerHour platform. They can either pay a down payment to get fixed price tasks done or contact experts to get custom projects done. You can manage all projects on the platform, receive payment and communicate with clients easily.

AngelList

AngelList is a platform for startups. The site has a list of thousands of full-time, part-time and remote work for skilled workers for many industries. With a single profile, you apply to many relevant startups. You can browse listed jobs by location, industry, salary, technology, and role.

Other sites you may find useful

Lesser known sites and apps you can use to find gig work include: Care (an app for care givers on-demand), Cavier (food delivery from local restaurants), Closet Collective (rent your clothing, shoes, bags and accessories for a fee), CrowdFlower (for data scientists who want to contribute to projects), Dolly (delivery or moving needs), DoorDash (food delivery service), Fancy Hands (US-based on-demand assistance work app), Handy (helps cleaners and handymen find work), HomeAway (rent your home to visitors to your town or city), SparcHire (on-demand finance and consulting work), TaskEasy (lawn care tasks for homeowners), Krop (helps tech freelancers find gigs), Remote (connects remote and freelancer workers with innovative companies), Envato Studio (a community of developers, designers and other creative professionals) and Crew (a network of designers and software developers selected to work on projects).

How to increase your chances of landing gigs

Create an ideal profile description

Your profile on a freelancing site is the most important marketing tool that can win projects for you. Put time into creating an ideal description about yourself that aims to pitch to a particular client instead of selling all your skills.

Personalize your description to fit every freelance site you sign for and focus on telling clients how your skill can help them. Don't create a service menu of everything you can do, but choose the most important skill for which you want to be known. Create a specific heading for every profile on gig work platforms. A winning title describes your skill in a few words, so be as precise as possible. This will help clients to understand what you offer as soon as they view your profile. Use Android Developer or iOS Developer, instead of Mobile Developer. Use a niche skill instead of a general skill. Target profiling can increase your chances of getting specific gigs, and your overall profitability.

In the short description of yourself, don't describe yourself in the third person; use the first-person pronoun. For example, instead of 'graphic designer with three years' experience in audio, text and image content creation' write 'I create amazing images that help you and your business attract and win customers.' Focus on how you can help clients succeed or solve problems. People looking for gig workers on freelancing sites are much more intrigued about your ability to solve their specific problems, and help them drive sales and results, rather than generic details of what you are capable of doing. In the short bio (preferably 300 words), prove to clients that you are qualified, capable and enthusiastic to take on a new project by mentioning how you have helped clients in the past. Don't forget to create a maintenance plan for your profiles. Just like a CV, it needs updating as you gain experience and work on projects, so revisit your profiles every six months to refresh them.

Boost your success with unique proposals

Many freelancing sites allow you to submit proposals for jobs that match your skill and you can increase your chances of winning projects if you focus on getting the details of every proposal right. Start every submission by carefully examining the description of the project and what you can do differently to solve specific problems. Do the scope and skills required to accomplish it match your expertise? Can you deliver on your promise when you consider your other commitments? How passionate are you about the task? It's better to be genuinely interested in taking on any project on a site before you submit your proposal. Enthusiasm can improve how you work and enhance your relationship with the client because you will fully commit to it. The benefits and compensation of a project may tempt you to submit proposals for many projects, but choose projects that will boost your skill, enhance your portfolio and get you closer to your goal of becoming an authority in your chosen niche. Working on an unsuitable project could delay and distract you from your long-term goal of establishing yourself as a credible expert.

If you are sure about submitting a proposal for a project, make it clear why you will do a better job than other freelancers. An updated profile and your introductory message to the prospective client should demonstrate the unique skill you bring and show similar and relevant assignments you have worked on in the past. Refer to Chapter 2 to learn how to create a successful portfolio. In every proposal, ask thoughtful questions related to the problem described in the job. Clearly outline how you intend to solve the problem and add a detailed timeline or milestones to show your work process. Avoid tweaking templates for your proposals, and write personal proposals that address details mentioned in the job description. Your terms of work should be concise and easy to digest. Prospective clients receive many proposals, so bids with long descriptions are likely to be skipped in favour of simple ones. Be precise about what you will offer, your fees, and how long you will take to complete it. Once you submit a proposal, be ready to respond quickly to questions clients may have about your bid.

You won't get a response from everybody, and you won't win every project you pitch for, so be prepared to make many bids on relevant projects. The initial unresponsiveness should not stop you from trying over and over again. For every pitch, do your research for new ways to convince clients of your ability to deliver, and make it personal. Proposal submission is a long-term commitment; success can take a couple of weeks or even months, so don't give up on your first try.

Key takeaways

- As technology improves and new options emerge, many people will have better opportunities to sell their services online no matter their location. Choosing the right online site to sell yourself or show your past work will become even more important.

- Your profile on a freelancing site is the most important marketing tool that can win projects for you. Put time into creating an ideal profile that aims to pitch a particular client instead of selling all your skills.

- When you choose to submit proposals on gig sites, clearly outline how you intend to solve the problem and add a detailed timeline or milestones to show your work process. Avoid tweaking templates for your proposals, and write personal proposals that address details mentioned in the job description.

11
Overcoming the fears of freelancing

We have already looked at the benefits of choosing to work for yourself and how you can build a reputable career as a gig worker. Yet many people see too many challenges and fear taking even a single step into the world of freelancing. Even for those who have recently started pitching themselves as independent consultants, the challenges of managing their professional lives can be overwhelming. This chapter will address common obstacles like making a decision to get started, and maintain the passion when you are a few months or a few years in as a gig worker.

The fear of getting started

Fear has a huge impact, especially when it comes to your life, work, your finances. What if I fail? What if I don't get clients? What if I don't make enough money to support my family? These are all real concerns that need to be addressed. Any life-changing journey can bring uncertainty, but with thoughtful preparation, your freelancing journey can be the most fulfilling decision of your life. Like all other decisions and actions you take in life, choosing to work for yourself requires a thoughtful plan. If you propose to leave your job to fully commit to an independent work career, or are thinking about starting a side project while remaining a full-time employee, you need to prepare yourself for a change of mindset. You have to plan for work, personal and financial responsibilities, and the commitments that will define your new career.

The fear of losing a regular pay cheque can be daunting, but it makes sense to have a few ideas or even projects that are already in the pipeline, and have saved up enough money to keep you going for a period of time when you are looking for clients. Regular bills like rent or a mortgage and all those direct debits going out every month need to be taken care of when you make the decision to fully commit to the freelance career. If you're giving up a regular salary, a complete plan of action and a clear picture of your income and outgoings should be undertaken. I never advise people to quit their jobs without realistic plans of how they intend to take care of themselves, their dependants (if any) and their business. A realistic financial plan should stretch to the next three months.

Many people choose not to work for themselves because they are worried about the details of setting up on their own, the current economic condition, their inabilities and everything else that can go wrong. To offset these understandable fears, you shouldn't jump into freelancing without a plan. Your plan should not just be limited to your finances, but should include what to include in your portfolio, how you intend to pitch clients, places to find gig work, the minimum number of pitches you can send every week, your responses to potential clients, contracts you can send to clients when you win their business, how to manage multiple projects and an actionable plan to upgrade your skills. Once you have this plan in place, make sure you know why you have chosen to work for yourself. Write down all the reasons why independent consulting is a viable career option for you. If you continue to feel the fear even after you have started, read the list and remind yourself why you pursued life as a freelancer.

Lack of confidence

The fear of not being good enough is one of the many reasons some people can't go into business. Your niche may be competitive, but it doesn't mean clients will choose not to work with you because you have little or no experience. Lack of confidence in yourself, the quality of your work, your ability to attract and retain clients, and managing your income can paralyze you and stop you from moving forward. Remember, the more projects you take on, no matter how small, the more experience you will build as an expert in your niche.

Once you choose to work for yourself, you need to realize that there are jobs for both new and highly skilled on-demand workers. No matter your level of experience, you can find the gig that's the right fit for you. What you need is confidence when you approach businesses for work.

To improve your confidence, start with projects that fully fit your expertise or small tasks or gigs that can help you build experience fast. It can help you relax whilst you approach clients, and will make you even more comfortable with new gigs you choose to work on.

If you don't feel confident in yourself you can hire a mentor or coach, take a course or use resources to help you build the courage you need to move forward. If you choose to hire a coach, find someone who is influential and has great connections. A good coach with a strong track record is likely to introduce you to his or her network, and the referral can improve your chances of getting more work because the clients know your coach.

You can also learn from other successful freelancers. Don't reinvent the wheel. There will be a lot of successful freelancers in your niche who share free tips for thriving as an independent worker. Read their stories about how they started, what they do differently to land clients, and everything they do to sustain themselves. In Chapter 12 I interview six successful freelancers who share their personal experiences and how they work. Use their lessons to make better decisions about how you work. You can even reach out to them to ask for advice.

Rejection

No matter how great you are at what you do, you won't win all prospective clients to whom you pitch. Every now and then you will be rejected, and that's acceptable. People and businesses have different needs and requirements and they turn down pitches for many reasons. For example, your pitch may get to the wrong person who is too busy to forward it to the right person, or the client may not have the budget for the project at the time of your pitch. In many cases, businesses and clients may not have the resources to support a new project or task.

The important thing is that you don't stop pitching. Reach out to potential clients through direct emails to decision makers, business events and responding to gig ads even if you keep getting rejections. The more you make yourself available for work, the faster you will be able to overcome the fear of rejection. No one likes to hear they are not the right fit for a task or project, but knowing how to pick yourself up and get back to pitching again is an important skill you need to grow and do well as a freelancer. Keep improving your pitches after every rejection, instead of worrying about your weaknesses.

Finding clients

The dreaded feeling that work might dry up at some point can be overwhelming. The thought of not finding reliable and long-term clients who can ensure consistent work can be defeating. Those anxious thoughts can stop you from trying anything new outside your comfort zone. An independent contractor has two major jobs. The first is to be amazing at what they do and the second is to find and retain clients. Whether you are planning to be a freelancer on the side or working as a full-time independent contractor, finding clients doesn't have to be impossible. Making that initial client contact takes time and attention, especially if you have not worked on any gig in the past. It can also be frustrating, just sending many cold emails without replies, or even securing that all-important first client. But once you take off, or, better still, as the client base increases with time and your portfolio and reputation in your industry grow, the journey is fulfilling and the sense of achievement totally outweighs the initial effort. When you consistently implement the ideas for finding work in the gig economy discussed in Chapter 4, you can position yourself to attract and find the right clients.

The mistake many freelancers make is that they stop looking for clients when their calendars are full with tasks or projects for a couple of weeks. Instead of waiting to complete projects before you begin looking for more work, keep looking for clients even when you are occupied. Don't get too comfortable when times are good and remember consistently to keep looking out for new opportunities. The more people you contact offering your services, the higher your chance of finding loyal clients you can work with. And the more clients you get, the better your chances of having a stable career. At some point, you won't need to market or promote yourself as hard as you will have done in the beginning. Many past clients will come to you with repeat business if you did a good job when they first engaged you.

It's hard to believe this when you are not there yet and it may sound impossible as a new gig worker, but trust me, so long as you don't give up, you will get to that point of your career. I used to apply for a lot of work almost every day in the past, but today my past clients consistently offer me work every month. I don't have to worry about lean or dry months without income.

Financial insecurity

Making enough money has been one of the biggest concerns for even full-time employees. Getting paid on time, saving enough money, and the fear that you won't be able to pay your bills can stop you from committing to the flexible on-demand working life. The fundamental question people ask about freelancing is whether it's possible to achieve financial stability. The answer is yes. You have more control over that than you might think. Drawing up a financial plan before you fully commit to self-employment can help you prepare for the future.

To live without financial insecurity, you need to learn how to budget and make saving a habit. In addition, if you have an emergency fund that covers at least six months' worth of outgoings it will help you focus on finding clients and building a business. Managing your money comes down to three key things:

- knowing how much you earn currently;
- managing your outgoings;
- establishing the best financial safety net.

Re-evaluate your expenses and reduce your wants (entertainment expenses) whilst you focus on your needs (necessary household bills). This will help you keep more money whilst you find your footing and increase your client base. Once you start working with clients, re-evaluate your income streams every quarter to find out how much you are bringing in, which strategies are working and what you should focus your energy on in order to bring in more clients. The key is not to get comfortable with a few clients but to keep improving how you attract and retain clients.

As you gain experience, it's also important to consider raising your rates. The fear for most freelancers is that, when they charge competitive rates, they will price themselves out of potential work. But the right price will improve your quality of clients, and increase your income in the long term. Low-budget work leads to wasted time and effort on more projects that don't necessarily lead to higher income. It also means you have to give up high-quality work that could lead to higher income in the future. Choose your work carefully.

Key takeaways

- The fear of getting started is real, but remember, every beginning is hard but not impossible. You are not helpless; you can overcome your fears with actionable steps, no matter how small.

- Getting started is an important step in building the freelancer career you want. Starting small and choosing the right projects will keep you motivated and allow you to expand your client base slowly in the coming months and years.

- If you plan to leave your job to fully commit to an independent work career or are thinking about starting a side project as a full-time employee, a complete plan of action and a clear picture of your incomings and outgoings is paramount.

- A great plan of action should not be limited to just your finances but should include how to find clients, places to register for gig work, competitive rates that will win high-quality clients, a working contract for clients and how to manage multiple projects.

- To improve your confidence, start with projects that fully fit your expertise or small tasks or gigs that can help you build experience fast. This will help you relax whilst you approach clients and you will be more comfortable with new gigs you choose to work on.

- The more you make yourself available for work, the faster you will be able to overcome the fear of rejection.

- Financial instability can be a huge cause of stress if you don't deal with it right from the beginning. A financial emergency plan, even before you fully commit to self-employment, can help you prepare for the future.

- Don't get too comfortable when times are good; consistently keep looking out for new opportunities when you start. The more people you contact offering your services, the higher your chance of finding loyal clients you can consistently work with. And the more clients you get, the better your chances of having a stable career.

12

Success stories of independent contractors

Building the life you want as a freelancer is like launching any business. You need all the advice and lessons you can get, especially from people who have already made it. When I decided to fully commit to life as an independent consultant, I read a lot about how to succeed when you choose to work for yourself. I consistently read success stories of people I admired and tried to apply all their advice and lessons to my life. To help you do exactly that and even more, I reached out to six successful contractors, and consultants who work for themselves. I asked them to share their typical day, how they promote themselves and find clients, the tools they consistently use for work, why they think some freelancers struggle to find clients, what you can do to improve your financial security, and what they would do differently if they were to start over. In this chapter successful independent contractors who have worked with companies and publishers including Microsoft, HSBC Bank, FedEx, Thinkific, Wall Street Journal, Harvard Business Review and Fast Company reveal what works for them and what you can do to thrive as a freelancer.

Paul Jarvis

Paul Jarvis is a designer and the author of *Everything I Know* and *Be Awesome at Online Business*. He is also the creator of three online courses: Creative Class, Chimp Essentials and Grow Your

Audience. He shares his story as an independent contractor, explains how he works, describes lessons learned along the way and offers advice on how to thrive when you choose to freelance.

Have you always worked for yourself?

At this point, yes. I've worked for myself for just about 20 years now. I spent a tiny bit of time in the corporate world, then at a design agency, but both were for less than a year combined.

What does a typical workday look like for you?

Each day I tend to have drastically different things to do. I also try to 'clump' similar work together, so I can get it done faster. On average, though, I wake up and clean out my inbox (typically 15–20 minutes), read the news (10–15 minutes) and get to work.

Tasks I tend to have to do each week include writing, design and code, and meetings/communication. I spend most of my time writing since I'm an author. I write weekly articles and also teach online courses. While technically my background is in design and development, and I still do both for my own projects, because I'm no longer working with clients or doing gigs, I don't get to do either for very long.

In terms of meetings/communication, because I work with a lot of people and get asked to do interviews, I spend a good deal of time talking. I always try to group calls together on Tuesday and Wednesday (and never on Monday or Friday). When I am writing, designing or coding I like to do those in long stretches of focused time – so no email open, no social media. I have no notifications on my phone or computer for anything. I like long stretches of time to work in, so I can get it done quickly.

What have you learned over the years about finding clients, marketing yourself and promoting your work?

Business at any level is human relationships. I got hired by Fortune 500 companies the same way that I got hired by Mom and Pop shops, which is because those people knew me through one degree of separation. So, I'm always working at keeping in touch with people I enjoy talking to and getting to know.

You never know who they know and, unless you're a sociopath, you should enjoy talking to and learning from others. Every business lead that's ever come my way has been because of spending time talking to and learning from others. As for marketing, I've always felt I'm a horrible sales person but a decent listener and I notice what people mean when they say what they say. So, for marketing, I always try to create my products based on what I hear others say they need, and word the sales copy using words other people use to describe the problem the product solves. I also spend a great deal of time keeping in touch with the people who are interested in my work. That's why I have a weekly newsletter where I share an article each Sunday. Those subscribers are the people who are interested in what I'm doing and what I have to say, so keeping in touch with them weekly means that my brand and products stay at the top of their minds.

For promoting, I always consider how my products help people, because business is serving others. Your business makes money when it serves others well, and when they get out (value) more than they feel they put in (money). So, when I'm promoting something I've created, I like to share how what I've made can help other people. And I make it as specific as possible because it's easier to sell something that's specially made for a certain audience.

What tools have you found to be consistently useful in your career, and why?

I'm not actually a huge fan of tools. I have almost no apps on my phone except for the default apps. With writing, I'm happy to write in any program. Same with design – I don't care if I'm using Photoshop or Sketch. I'd rather spend more time refining my skills than think about how specific tools work, since tools change all the time.

That said, the internet does make it ridiculously easy to keep in touch with large numbers of people. For example, my mailing list is over 30,000 subscribers, and I can email that many people just as easily as I can email one person, using MailChimp (that said, if MailChimp disappeared tomorrow, I'd move to another platform). It's also very easy to sell or collect money online now using things like Stripe, Paypal or Braintree. I remember in the 1990s when it required so much work and took so much time to set up even simple e-commerce. For platforms, I tend to stay away from social media. I've never been on Facebook or LinkedIn and I only use Twitter as an outlet for sarcasm. I'd rather focus on my own platform: my list and my website. That way, I have absolute control over them. I wouldn't want to rely on a platform that could change the rules or charge me to reach my audience there.

Why do you think many freelancers fail to succeed and have difficulties finding work?

There's a difference between having a skill and running a business. So, a great designer won't automatically be a great freelancer since much of freelancing is business. When I was a freelancer, I would be lucky if I got four hours a day to design. The rest of the time was spent running the business: chasing leads, closing sales, doing marketing, keeping my books in order, dealing with my lawyer, scheduling projects, etc. Freelancing is a business. If it's not treated like one, you're going to fail.

Financial insecurity is a huge problem for many people who choose to work for themselves. How do you plan financially without that security?

I feel tremendously secure. Many people I know who've had corporate jobs have been let go or laid off or downsized or simply moved on many, many times in the last 20 years and I've always had the same job and same employer (myself). I get to call the shots and manage things, so it's up to me to make sure things are secure.

That said, freelancers have to save more. We don't get employer-funded retirement plans or even healthcare coverage. I've always put as much money away as possible and lived below my means as much as possible to build up my savings as quickly as possible.

Since I'm not an investor, I don't want to think about my money, but I want it to grow. To me, that's security. I invest in both my own business (which has a high rate of return) but also in index funds, so I can see my money grow at a higher rate than inflation. When I started, my savings buffer wasn't very big, but every month I would add more to it. After a few years, I had more savings than most of my friends in 'real' jobs. That felt pretty secure to me.

If you were to start all over again, what would you do differently and why?

I would have learned more about business. When I started, I had the skill but not the business smarts or sense, so I lost a lot of money on stupid things. I wouldn't have even gone to school for business, but I would have read more books, learned from others, and tried to pick up as much as I could from those around me. I also would have implemented immediate payment on receipt of invoice for clients on day one – that would have saved a lot of headaches and late/missed payments.

What are your thoughts on the future of work?

It's easier to work for yourself now, because of technology. Things we can do today on a cheap computer weren't even possible 20 years ago. That doesn't mean we're better workers now, though; it just means we can be crappy workers from anywhere in the world and not in an office. So, the future of work still means figuring out how to be productive, focused and profitable.

Are you working on anything at the moment that you want us to know about?

I have a new book coming out called *Company of One* that focuses on how businesses can get better without being bigger. It comes out 15 January 2019.

Where can we find your work?

My newsletter, The Sunday Dispatches: https://pjrvs.com

Jessica Greene

Jessica is a freelance writer. She creates content for business-to-business companies – typically, startups and agencies. Jessica writes long-form blog content, case studies, eBooks and white papers for business both small and large. She used to be a writing instructor and corporate marketer.

Have you always worked for yourself?

No. I worked as a freelance writer for a couple of years while I was in college, but after I graduated I ventured into the world of full-time employment. I worked for other people for nearly a decade, including major corporations, local businesses, and tech startups. I learned a lot over that decade. I took the skills I learned at each job and expanded on them in the next. I wouldn't change how I spent that time in my career because it's been integral to my success as a freelancer. But, at the end of the day, working for others just wasn't for me. With every year that passed, I felt more and more compelled to re-launch my freelancing career. And two years ago I decided that the time had come. I left my full-time job and have been working for myself ever since.

What does a typical workday look like for you?

When I read about self-employment, people always talk about being able to work whenever they want, wherever they want. 'On the beach' is a pretty common phrase. But my typical workday is much less exotic. I work from 8 am to 5 pm Monday through Friday. I mostly work in my home office while sitting at my desk, though sometimes I'll post up on the couch if I don't need two monitors.

Why so boring? Well, it's partly out of the habit of working for others for ten years, and partly because I have a daughter who's in middle school and a husband with a typical nine-to-five job. A traditional schedule just makes more sense for me and my family. But I think the idea of working whenever, wherever is just a way of describing the freedom that comes with working for yourself.

For me, that freedom is not being chained to a computer when I don't have any work to do. When I finish my work, I'm done for the day. It's not having to ask for permission to go to the doctor. It's being able to pick my daughter up after school every day.

What have you learned over the years about finding clients, marketing yourself and promoting your work?

In my experience, the best way to market yourself is to get your name on things. When I first started out, I took mostly ghost-writing assignments. It made finding new work incredibly difficult. I had no personal brand, and new clients basically had to trust that I had actually written the samples I sent because the by-lines were never my own. That alone was a huge hurdle. Plus, I spent an incredible amount of time looking for and applying for gigs. After I decided to stop ghost-writing and only work for clients willing to give me a by-line, that all changed. People see my work on other sites and reach out to me directly with offers for work. And the amazing thing is that the sites I write for don't even include a link to my website or my email address. People actually have to search to find my website or one of my social profiles.

Having a way for people to find you is also key to promoting yourself. All freelancers need a website, even if it's a very basic one, and one or two business-focused profiles on social networking sites. I emphasize one or two because it's impossible for one person to maintain a presence on too many channels. Outdated and neglected profiles don't inspire confidence. Beyond that, I deliver my clients my best work, on time, every time. They reward me with more work – sometimes for their own companies, and sometimes in the form of referrals.

What tools have you found to be consistently useful in your career and why?

A lot of the tools I use are very industry-specific, so I'll focus on those with a wider audience. I use QuickBooks Self-Employed for bookkeeping. It automatically pulls transactions from my business account, so I never forget to record any income or expenses. It calculates how much I owe in quarterly taxes, so I'm never hit with late payment penalties. It automatically populates my tax returns with all of my expense data, which saves me a lot of time during tax season.

I use Mint for my personal budget. It lets me set my target spending in different categories (groceries, entertainment, bills, etc) and track my progress towards those spending goals each month. Early on in my freelancing career, I made the mistake of thinking I didn't need a budget. Now, Mint is the first app I open every morning. I use Trello to track my work. It gives me a complete picture of what work I have in the pipeline and when assignments are due. All of my clients use

Trello, too. It a great tool for collaborating across large and distributed teams – and also a great tool for managing a personal to-do list.

Why do you think many freelancers fail to succeed and have difficulties finding work?

I don't personally know any freelancers who've failed to succeed, so all I can do is offer my best guesses based on the things I've struggled with as a freelancer. I mentioned earlier that I was a freelancer while I was in college but took full-time roles after graduating. Part of the reason why I stopped freelancing was because I just didn't have the discipline to turn freelancing into a career at that point in my life. When you work for yourself, you have to be incredibly self-disciplined. No one's watching to make sure I'm at my desk at 8 am every morning. No one's monitoring my internet activity to see if I'm spending too much time on Facebook. I'm at home with constant access to all of my toys and hobbies, and without self-discipline those distractions can easily lead to failure.

In my mid-twenties I lacked the self-discipline needed for successful self-employment. But after working full time for ten years, exercising my self-discipline is second nature. It's possible that some freelancers fail simply because the freedom is too tempting and distracting. I don't think that's a bad thing. It's certainly something people can overcome. I think the other big pitfall is falling into the traps of fear or nostalgia. Sometimes you don't have enough work, and you start to worry that you'll never have enough work again.

Sometimes paying quarterly taxes hurts, and you start fantasizing about the days when the money just came out of your pay cheque magically so you never had to miss it. In those moments, it's easier to call it quits and find a full-time job. It's harder to have patience and optimism and stay the course.

I've found a few things help when things get hard. First, don't leave your full-time job until you've saved enough money to get by for six months with no income. Second, save for a rainy day. Your situation can change in an instant as a freelancer. The best way to keep those moments from becoming failures is to have money in the bank to rely on. Third, surround yourself with supportive people who understand why you do what you do. I'm blessed with a wonderful husband who talks sense into me when I decide I'm fed up. Take advantage of the support friends and family can provide.

Financial insecurity is a huge problem for many people who choose to work for themselves. How do you plan financially without that security?

I know exactly how much money I need to cover all of my monthly expenses. I make sure I always have enough recurring work to (at minimum) cover those expenses. I have a strict budget set up in Mint, and I never go over what I've budgeted. I pick up one or two one-off projects each month, and I put that income into savings. This way, if something changes with my ongoing work – or if I have an unexpected expense – I have something to fall back on.

If you were to start all over again, what would you do differently and why?

I wouldn't start over again. I'm exactly where I want to be and wouldn't change anything.

What are your thoughts on the future of work?

I think the trend towards self-employment will change all types of employment for the better. The perks of self-employment will inevitably make companies who want to hire people full time rethink their expectations. For example, I spent so many hours as a full-time employee just staring at a computer screen. Even though my work was finished, I was still expected to sit at my desk until 5 pm. As a freelancer, when I'm finished with work, I'm free to do whatever I want. And that's how things should be. If we're doing what we're expected to do, it shouldn't matter when we do it or how long it takes.

There are exceptions, of course. Retail workers and customer service representatives obviously need to be available even if no customers currently need assistance. But for knowledge workers, the old rules of the workplace are becoming irrelevant. And I think in order to attract people away from self-employment companies will have to write new rules. I think – and I hope – that will be a good thing for the workplace of the future.

Where can we find your work?

I'm a regular contributor to a few different blogs and an occasional contributor to a few others. Instead of listing them all – and since parts of that list could be outdated before this is published – I'll just say that the best way to see my newest pieces is to follow me on Twitter (@JessGreeneMktg). Any time I have a new piece published, I post a link to it there.

Joe Mullich

Joe is a copywriter. His work has been featured in popular publications including the *Wall Street Journal*, *Wired*, *Forbes*, *Harvard Business Review* and *American Express*. Joe has written for many Fortune 500 companies like Microsoft, FedEx, HSBC Bank, Ford Motor Company and top advertising firms.

Have you always worked for yourself?

After graduating from college I worked at a public relations company, magazine, and newspaper. I had about six years working for others before I struck out on my own, which I have done for 20 years. I am a self-employed writer who produces books, scripts, magazine articles and corporate material.

What does a typical workday look like for you?

I bike to Starbucks where I pull out my laptop and start working around 9. I usually knock off around 4:30 pm and go to the gym. I find that the noise and hubbub of the coffee shop keep me more energetic than working in isolation from home. I used to keep bankers' hours but my schedule has become more fluid. The work I do on a given day can vary significantly depending on projects and deadlines. I might research, conduct interviews, write or have meetings. On a typical day, I am working on several projects, both long-term and short-term.

What have you learned over the years about finding clients, marketing yourself and promoting your work?

It's important to understand the market. Many freelance writers have little appreciation for the types of clients and type of material that is in demand. Even if you choose to produce lesser-paying material, because it provides greater satisfaction and you enjoy it more, that should be a choice you make based on knowledge of the marketplace.

It's important to understand the needs of clients. While the world seems to have an overabundance of writers, many clients have difficulty finding writers who can produce the material they want on a consistent basis. Any type of marketing should speak to the potential customer based on their needs and their pains. This is marketing 101 but it's staggering how so many freelancers talk in terms of 'me, me, me' rather than 'you, you, you'.

It's important to put your personality on display in your marketing. People like to work with people they like. I write a blog about my experience hanging out at Starbucks, and the interactions I have with people there. I linked to the blog on my website. Many clients who approach me about completely different types of writing, like technology topics, often remark on the blog because it is funny and unusual. Good marketing takes chances and stands out. In the past, I have approached clients with direct mail packages that include a quiz with the headline 'Are the Freelance Writers You're Using Competent?' The quiz provides a funny (and provocative) way for me to tout my own skills and it's gotten me a lot of business – people figure if I can write effectively and cleverly for myself, I can do the same for them.

What tools have you found to be consistently useful in your career and why?

LinkedIn: every year lots of people find me there. It's critical to have an appealing LinkedIn profile. Mine is https://www.linkedin.com/in/joemullich/. Rather than use a dull title like 'writer,' I describe myself as 'Story Teller: Specializing in Words, Compellingly Arranged.'

A dedicated website with your own URL – even if people find you through different means, they will always check you out on your website. It's important for the site to be appealing and professional, but it should also show who you are as a person. In my site (joemullich.com) I include standard elements like samples and client testimonials, but I also link to my blog and have a page about my interest in the outdoors and volunteer work I do.

Why do you think many freelancers fail to succeed and have difficulties finding work?

Many freelancers are skilled in producing a product or service and enjoy their work. But they don't enjoy the process of finding work and don't approach it with creativity or enthusiasm. Many freelance writers, understandably, want to do the kind of writing they enjoy, without giving much thought to what types of writing the marketplace values. The types of writing that people find the most fun, like travel writing, are typically crowded and low-paying.

Or they look for work on websites that require bids, where the pay is often dreadful. In the writing field, in particular, it's quite easy to be overwhelmed with work while going broke because the work is unprofitable. It's the equivalent of starving to death as you fill your face with food that has no nutritional value. Writers, and freelancers in general, have often never sold anything, so they don't know how to go about selling their work.

Financial insecurity is a huge problem for many people who choose to work for themselves. How do you plan financially without that security?

The first thing to realize is that financial insecurity is not limited to self-employed people. If you have a full-time job, you can be fired at any moment. As a freelancer, there are many ways to build stability. Diversify your client base. Diversify the type of products you produce. Look for clients who have an ongoing stream of work rather than one-offs. This is a personal choice, but I would also say to live frugally. It always puzzles me why so many people put unnecessary stress on themselves by buying things they don't need that give them no pleasure.

If you were to start all over again, what would you do differently and why?

If I were starting now, I would have approached the writing business in a more entrepreneurial manner. When I was starting out, the common approach was to find clients (magazines, companies etc) who would give you jobs. Today, I would cut out the middleman and develop websites where I reached readers directly. In that way, I would develop my own customer base, which would give me a greater opportunity to scale and make passive income. The trouble with traditional freelancer writing is that it is more akin to a job than a business – you only make money when you produce new material, and there are only so many hours in the day to produce that material.

What are your thoughts on the future of work?

The freelance writing world has always been in flux, but the state of change has dramatically increased. People who aren't anticipating the future are already behind.

Where can we find your work?

Joemullich.com

Emmeline Pidgen

Emmeline Pidgen is an illustrator specializing in creating books, advertising, comics, and live illustration. Emmeline was the winner of UK Freelancer of the Year award in 2016 and has worked with clients like Tesco, Egmont Publishing, and Jessica Kingsley Publishing/Hachette. Emmeline is currently writing and illustrating her first graphic novel, as well as working on a new edition of her guide for creative freelancers.

What does a typical workday look like for you?

One of the great things about being freelance is that every day can be as different as you want it to be. I don't tend to have a rigid schedule or routine, although I do make to-do lists and goal plans for the coming week, with stricter structures for commission deadlines. It's good to have structure, but enough freedom to work on what's driving you creatively at the time. Inspiration is not something you can really force, so when I get stuck in a rut with a project I'll switch to doing some other drawing, clear my head with a walk, or step into a totally different world through reading. Most often you'll find me working in my studio on a commission in the morning (usually book illustration or advertising), and in the afternoon I spend time developing my own work illustrating and writing graphic novels, picture books and stand-alone pieces.

What have you learned over the years about finding clients, marketing your work and promoting yourself?

Whilst running my illustration business, I've learned that it's not only vital for your portfolio to be perfect and readily available, but it's so incredibly important to build genuine connections and support other freelancers. A slick website, a gorgeous portfolio, and an impressive client list can be very beneficial, but it's getting to know people, being truly supportive of others, and dropping the hard-sell to actually talk to people that will take you the furthest.

Where can we find your work?

www.emmelineillustration.com

Sid Bharath

Sid is an entrepreneur and software-as-a-service marketing consultant. He works with software startups to help them identify their best growth channels and scale up in a data-driven and systematic manner. Sid has worked at or consulted for Thinkific, LemonStand, CartHook, Crazy Egg, Flippa, Edloud, Push Operations, etc.

Have you always worked for yourself?

Not always. I've spent a lot of time working at various companies. I was a software developer at Yahoo, and a consultant at Deloitte before I first worked for myself. I tried starting a couple of businesses, before moving into freelance marketing. After a couple of years of that, I went back to a job, this time running marketing for startups like Thinkific and Lemonstand. I recently started working for myself again, after helping Thinkific achieve rapid growth, as a growth marketing consultant for other software companies.

What does a typical workday look like for you?

The day starts with me reading a book for a bit while having coffee. Then I head to the gym, and after I come back it's down to work. The work always changes, depending on the client. I could be creating a new ad for one client, getting on a call with another, and putting together a proposal for a new client.

What have you learned over the years about finding clients, marketing yourself and promoting your work?

There's definitely a balance between doing work for clients, and also promoting yourself to find more clients. One thing I've learned is that nothing works better for marketing yourself than previous results. I created a bit of a name for myself because of my work at Thinkific and got interviewed on a few popular blogs and podcasts because of that. And some personal connections I made in the past have been my source of clients. This might sound controversial, but I think there are so many freelancers out there who haven't got enough experience under their belt. I see all these Facebook ads for 'gurus' who run ads for clients but they've only ever taken some online course about it. If you don't have much real-world experience, get some by working at a company for a few years.

What tools have you found to be consistently useful in your career and why?

A calendar scheduling tool like Calendly is extremely helpful to book meetings with clients. Skype or Zoom is great for one-on-one calls with clients, Evernote for note-taking, Grammarly because spelling mistakes are bad, and Bonsai to help manage projects and proposals.

Why do you think many freelancers fail to succeed and have difficulties finding work?

For one, it's the inexperience I mentioned earlier. Also, I think too many offer the same service that everyone else is and there's no differentiation. You have to niche down. For example, there are so many marketers out there, but there are very few growth-oriented marketers who specialize in SAAS, which is why I can find clients and charge premium prices.

Financial insecurity is a huge problem for many people who choose to work for themselves. How do you plan financially without that security?

I track my finances to make sure I'm saving money each month, but I don't really plan much. I know that I'll always be able to find clients, and I don't need too many to make a good living because I charge premium prices. Besides, worst-case scenario, I can always go back to working at another company because of the work experience I've built up.

If you were to start all over again, what would you do differently and why?

I don't really know if I'd change much but if I really had to say something, it would be that I'd not get into marketing and would work in artificial intelligence instead. That's the future.

What are your thoughts on the future of work?

I think work is definitely going to change because most things will get automated. Lots of people will see their jobs get automated. Countries are already preparing for this by testing universal basic income. It's important to keep up to date with what's happening with technology because though many jobs will be lost to automation, there will be new ones to build and manage the things that do the automation.

Are you working on anything new at the moment?

I'm working on a new program that I can offer to marketers and founders at small startups to help them figure out their most effective growth channels and how to scale those up. I'm still in the planning stages of it.

Where can we find your work?

You can find my website here – sidbharath.com. I'm also on LinkedIn – linkedin.com/in/sidbharath.

Ilise Benun

Ilise Benun is the founder of Marketing-Mentor.com, a resource site for creative professionals. Ilise developed and delivered programming for creative professionals for almost 30 years. She is the author of seven business books for the 'creatively self-employed,' and the co-founder/host of the HOW Design Live podcast.

Have you always been a mentor?

Actually, this month marks the thirtieth anniversary of my being fired from my second job after college, and I decided I would never work for anyone else again. I was angry and ignorant and a little impetuous and so I just started. So, I never had a dream of what I wanted to do and it certainly was not to be a mentor. But what I have learned to preach, if you will, is that everything flows from the market and the market will tell you what it needs. And if you have what it needs you can provide it. And so, when I got fired, I looked around at all my friends in New York and they were all creative people who needed help getting organized, and so I just said I could do that, so I started helping them get organized. And then it was clear that underneath all the papers there was always something that had to do with marketing and self-promotion that they weren't doing. So, I said well let's do that, let's give the person the information they're asking for, let's go to the trade show and get you ready for it, or let's put together a brochure, and so it just evolved.

Helping people do it seemed like I could begin advising and mentoring people on what worked so I very slowly and not particularly consciously made that transition to mentoring and I think part of it is also that I've been mentored very well and so I've learned by being on the other side of the fence. And so, it's not like I wanted to be a mentor but I definitely have learned how to guide people and customize the suggestions so that people get exactly what they need when they need it, instead of 'you could read my book and get all the information'.

What does a typical workday look like for you?

I don't like routine, so every day is different. That's one of the benefits of being self-employed. Every day can be different. My days are spent on the phone consulting and mentoring with clients all day long, with little breaks to walk my dog. And some days I leave totally open so that I can think and rate everything I learn while I'm working with my clients.

What have you learned over the years about finding clients, marketing yourself and promoting your work?

Well, the best marketing thing of all is networking. My definition of networking is meeting people in person, in real time. And asking questions and learning about them. And being able to make an impression, which is very difficult to do. It takes a lot of time, but if you're in person with someone it's a lot easier because there's a physical presence involved and so I find for myself. That's why I'm going to the HOW conference next week in Boston because that gives me a week to network and talk to people and see what's going on and see how I can help and see what the trends are and see what the needs are. That's really one of the best ways to get the information you need to be constantly reinventing yourself or your services. The problem many people have with networking is that they don't know what to say. They focus on themselves when really the focus should be on the other person and what you can learn from other people. I approach networking with curiosity, which means in a practical way, preparing a list of questions that can help me start conversations. For example, how is your business and what's working for you lately or what's your biggest problem or challenge at the moment? Ask questions related to the kind of work that you do and can offer.

What tools have you found to be consistently useful in your career and why?

One of the best tools is the ability to say no and be really focused. Many people are not clear about what they're trying to accomplish and what it takes to get there, but if you can clarify that, then that is your focus and you don't need anything else. What I'm looking for are creative professionals and LinkedIn is a good resource for finding them.

Why do you think many freelancers fail to succeed and have difficulties finding work?

This has a lot to do with focus and knowing what you're offering, and to find clients in real life, in real time, at an event and talking to them. And if you don't find the right people, then keep looking. Many people who complain are not actually looking hard enough. If you look strategically, you can usually find what you're looking for, but I think people give up too easily. People also like to complain. Leave every event with the contact information of the people you met, follow up, usually through email, but you could use a combination of email and LinkedIn and maybe even snail mail to remind them of the conversation that you had and what you learned from them. It's not always so much about pitching what you have to offer. Ask questions about the problems people have that you could then offer to solve.

Financial insecurity is a huge problem for many people who choose to work for themselves. What is the best way creative professionals can manage their finances without that security of a job?

Regular income is possible. Either you have a lot of prospects or a lot of projects in your pipeline that are ready to go at all times. That requires a lot of marketing.

If you're going for the regular income where clients pay you on a monthly basis for something that you do over a period of time as opposed to a one-shot type of work, then you have to figure out what those projects are and the clients who need them. You can also choose work based on fixed fees. I'm not a big fan of being paid by time, whether it's hourly or daily. But, in general, fixed ongoing projects are better for everyone because you can regulate your cash flow, you know how much you're going to be paid and they know how much they're going to pay you; but you have to be able to estimate accurately in order to do that. Also, getting paid quickly means asking to be paid more or choosing clients and prospects who will pay according to your terms.

Any advice for new freelancers?

Have a plan, because it always takes longer to get established than you think. I'm not the type of person that says 'just do it'. If you're not prepared then it's not going to work out, so my advice is be serious, put some money away and start on the side. I wouldn't advise anybody to quit their job until they have a serious plan of action.

Where can we find more information about your books and mentorship programme?

On my online store: www.marketing-mentor.com. I always have new products, new downloads and marketing plans. Right now, I'm working on a new one to help people price their services better.

13
The future of the gig economy

Work is evolving beyond the limits of working just for one person or organization. Today, technology has made it possible to find and work for clients and employers at almost any geographic location. People have more career options now than ever. The rise of gig workers is redefining making a living in the 21st century. For anyone who feels frustrated by the inflexibility at a traditional workplace, gig work offers more opportunities to generate income at your own pace. The gig economy has opened up a lot of opportunities for people from all backgrounds and different locations. And it has enabled businesses to hire short-term talent from practically anywhere in the world. In this chapter we will discuss how the gig economy will change how work is done today, what will change in the next five or ten years and possibly beyond, why you need to embrace the gig economy, and what to expect as you choose to be a gig worker.

The future is freelance

The freelance economy is gradually becoming the economy. Think about how people used to work 20 years ago. Compare that to the way experts deliver value to both businesses and consumers today. The two scenarios are very different. Businesses processes are now faster and more dynamic, and employment is getting more flexible. *The Intuit 2020 Report* predicts that 'the long-term trend of hiring contingent workers will continue to accelerate with more than

80 per cent of large corporations planning to substantially increase their use of a flexible workforce' (Strutz, 2016). The report antici- pates that over 40 per cent of the working population in the US alone (or 60 million people) will be working for themselves by the year 2020. Businesses are creating new opportunities for freelanc- ers to join them as they seek fresh talent to help them build better products and deliver excellent customer services. Freelancers are not hired by startups and small-sized businesses alone: major multi- national companies with thousands of regular full-time employees engage the services of expert freelancers for specific projects and tasks.

According to Flexjobs (one of largest part-time, freelance and flexible job sites), BBC Worldwide, Intel, Accenture, Affirm, Rover, Kaplan and GoPro were among companies that hired the most free- lancers on their platform from April through July 2017 (Jay, 2017). Freelancers from different backgrounds are providing innovative solutions and new perspectives for businesses of all sizes. 'Microsoft has nearly two-thirds as many contractors as full-time employees,' says Tad Milbourn of TechCrunch, an online publisher of technol- ogy industry news, (Milbourn, 2015). Highly skilled independent workers will continue to be in high demand as even more large corporations recruit on-demand workers to join their workforce. The advances in technology continue to lead to an ever-evolving team on the same project, virtual offices across the world, and a new way to hire short-term workers. The progress of technological tools allows businesses of all sizes to tap into the brightest minds globally.

Technology alone is not the only factor that has helped break down conventional work patterns and promote a shift towards more favourable work conditions for independent workers. Other factors like uncertain economic conditions, the need to supplement income and the craving for a better work–life balance and quality of life have contributed to the growth of freelance and consulting work. These factors will continue to make change the new constant for people who have embraced gig work. Whatever the motivation for flexible work, the gig economy is poised for consistent growth globally. The constant upward evolution of the global workforce means that winners of the future economy will be those who will embrace change and adapt.

The soaring growth of talent sites will continue to make it easy for freelancers to choose to work with businesses on their own terms and from anywhere that fits their lifestyle. Traditional key decision-making positions in large and established corporations are not likely to be given to remote workers, because these businesses need key managers to meet in person every now and then to make important decisions about business growth and direction. But as workers continue to pursue new careers that support their specific life, businesses will make room for the new, modern workforce that will change the perception of work and what it means to make a living in the future.

The changing face of job descriptions

Many companies have invested in structures that allow employees to move up the career ladder based on past performance and contribution to the growth of the business. Typically, in an established company, work is categorized into specific descriptions with performance indicators and reward packages. But as people continue to place emphasis on the accumulation of experiences, work–life balance, flexibility and improvement of skills, employers are beginning to shift from carefully planned structures that reward just performance to helping their productive workforce find fulfilment at work. The relentless pace of change in the workplace is necessitating new rules of engagement.

In the modern work environment of the future, many companies will organize business processes into projects and hire the best talent to work on short-term deliverables. This will allow businesses to focus on tangible results instead of monitoring effort, activity or diligence to the process. Employers will think in terms of specialisms. John Boudreau, co-author of *Lead the Work*, writes, 'Job descriptions usually describe work performed by full-time employees, throwing together a series of skills and requirements that seem large enough for an employment contract' (Boudreau, 2015). In his argument in favour of the deconstruction of work, Boudreau says that regular full-time employment is only one way to get work done. Work can be managed in a way that involves the brightest minds you can put together instead of relying on just full-time employees. Work won't be just a job description as companies continue to embrace and hire talented remote gig workers. But it's important to note that job types will evolve differently.

Some deliverable-oriented tasks, including software development, designing, accounting, marketing, writing and customers support, can easily be transitioned to gig roles, but other business management roles or people management responsibilities will continue to be performed by in-house full-time employees.

Accenture, a global management consulting and professional services firm, says that freelance is the future. The company predicts that in the next ten years the world will witness new Global 2000 companies (annual top 2,000 public companies in the world ranked by *Forbes* magazine) with no full-time employees outside of the C-suite (chief executive officer, chief financial officer, chief operating officer and chief information officer). Instead, companies will focus on investing in what they call a 'liquid workforce'. This may sound unimaginable to a lot of people, but it suggests that the future of full-time roles lies in strategic high-level decision-making roles that affect the direction of the business. Highly talented and credible independent contractors will be hired to support managers run businesses. 'The liquid workforce is rapidly becoming the new normal for how businesses organize themselves. Traditional methods cannot keep up with the pace of change in the digital age and forward-thinking businesses are already beginning to learn that their workforce strategy has the potential to be a major competitive advantage,' reports Accenture (Technology Vision, 2016). Ultimately, many businesses will consist of owners, C-suite officers, talent hunters, flexible workers and independent workers.

In the future, talent platforms will get smarter and automatically find, apply or match contractors with suitable and relevant talent hunters when they have an opening on their calendars. Entire project team members could be assembled with the click of a button. As companies increase the percentage of short-term contractors they work with, and the competition for top freelancer contractors becomes high, established businesses will create remote talent development structures that will provide career enhancement opportunities for frequent contractors. Others will try to improve their chances of working with the most creative minds by providing the best tools and support for their contingent workers. The implications of this shift are enormous, but in the long term a more dynamic and results-oriented economy will emerge.

The gradual shift from CVs to portfolios

People have presented themselves in the form of CVs for years. These provide a linear view of what they used to do and which companies they worked for and positions they held. The focus of a CV has always been about the quantity of experience in the past. But that is changing. In the modern world of work, businesses and clients will value your achievements, tangible results of your past work and your personal initiatives. Portfolios are not just a collection work for creative professionals; anyone looking to thrive in the new world of work can make one. A portfolio is a comprehensive view of your professional abilities, and how you can contribute to the success of any prospective client. What businesses and clients are looking for in people they want to hire is changing from 'who you've worked for' to 'what you've done' and how you have used your skills in the past. Prepare yourself for the future by creating a collection of your work that reflects what you want to be known for, and make it compelling. You can increase the visibility of your portfolio and boost your chances of getting found by prospective clients with photos, videos, links to your work, presentation slides and recommendations. Soon, people will have not only LinkedIn profiles, but also measurements of what they are good at and how creative they are.

A greater need for networking

Independent contractors do not work in isolation. Referrals still play a key role in attracting and retaining new customers. Business is human, and your connections can improve how you find clients. As demand for freelancers surge in the future, who you are connected to, especially when you are building experience, will become very important for your career. Companies want to work with people they can trust. Better networking can often lead to bigger projects, often even before a formal project is posted on gig sites. Sometimes, your online portfolio is impersonal to convince prospective clients to engage your services, as some people do business with contractors who are already in their network. Connecting with other freelancers, meeting them for relevant events, recommending them for other gigs you can't take up can open up a lot of other opportunities for you in the future. If you are not sociable, find resources to help you improve your networking skills. That can help you spot networking opportunities daily.

Networking doesn't just happen at relevant events. It can be as simple as having a casual conversation, asking to stay in touch, following up in a friendly way and providing value to the people you meet. It's not about forcing a business card into the hand of every person you meet. You might offer to take your new contacts out for coffee, listen to what they do, how they fare and even learn from them. This can help you strengthen your relationship with them. If anything comes up in their network that relates to what you do, they are more likely to recommend you. People are more inclined to work with people who their connections or friends have already praised for delivering great results. In the future, freelancers who don't treat others as competition will thrive and win more clients. Consistent work will largely depend on the connections you've forged throughout your career.

The future of work

A connected future, where labour can be hired from anywhere in the world regardless of their location, is already here. It's now more important than ever to reinvent your skills and position yourself as an expert in your industry. Today, over 34 per cent of businesses, both small and large, engage contract workers for more than 12 months or longer, according to research by Ernst & Young (2016). To survive in the modern world of work, businesses adapt their company culture to attract and work with the smartest minds. The workforce of the future expects employers and clients to embrace business tools that make work efficient and collaboration among people from different locations better. They will have to offer their workforce more than a great salary to attract and retain top minds; they'll need to create opportunities for people to make a meaningful impact through work.

People are increasingly choosing to work independently. In the survey by Ernst & Young, 25 per cent of businesses expect to use over 30 per cent of contingent workers for various tasks and business processes by 2020 (Ernst & Young, 2016). You have the edge to put technology to work in your favour as it becomes more robust and opens more doors for your career. As many companies open up to work with workers from all over the world, you can not only create work opportunities to increase your income but also find work that brings meaning and purpose into your life. The digital revolution is not leading to a cold future where robots take over your work – it is opening up avenues for human empowerment where you will firmly be in control of your working life.

In *The Future of Work: A journey to 2022* by Pricewaterhouse-Coopers (PwC), 10,000 people in the US, Germany, the UK, China and India were asked to give their opinions on the future of work and how it will affect their future. Sixty-six per cent of them thought the future world of work will be promising and full of possibilities. They believed they would be successful. Fifty-three per cent thought technological breakthroughs would transform the way people work over the next five to ten years, (PWC, 2014). Your success at work in the future will depend on your ability to embrace and harness change, and employers who invest in the resources to empower both their full-time and contingent workers will work with some of the brightest minds in their industries.

Key takeaways

- The freelance economy is gradually becoming the new economy.

- Improvement in technology continues to help companies find and hire on-demand gig workers across the world. It continues to lead to an ever-evolving team on the same project, virtual offices across the world and a new way to hire short-term workers.

- The soaring growth of talent sites will continue to make it easy for freelancers to choose to work with businesses on their own terms and from anywhere that fits their lifestyle.

- In the modern work environment of the future, many companies will organize business processes into projects and hire the best talent to work on short-term deliverables that allow businesses to focus on tangible results instead of monitoring effort, activity or diligence to the process.

- As online flexible work platforms evolve, they will get smarter and automatically find, apply or match contractors with suitable and relevant talent hunters when they have an opening on their calendars. Entire project teams could be assembled with the click of a button.

- In the future, freelancers who don't treat others as competition will thrive and win more clients. Consistent work will largely depend on the connections you've forged throughout your career.

- In the modern world of work, businesses and clients will value your achievements, tangible results of your past work and your personal initiatives.

- Prepare yourself for the future by creating a collection of your work that reflects what you want to be known for, and make it compelling.

- The improvement and advancement of technology for work is not leading to a cold future where robots take over your work. Instead, it's opening up avenues for human empowerment where you will firmly be in control of your working life.

References

Boudreau, J (2015) It's time to blow up job descriptions, 19/09 [Online] www.cornerstoneondemand.com/rework/its-time-blow-job-descriptions

Ernst & Young (2016) Global contingent workforce study, April [Online] gigeconomy.ey.com/Current-state/Key-insights

Intuit (2010) *Intuit 2020 Report: Twenty trends that will shape the next decade*, October [Online] http-download.intuit.com/http.intuit/CMO/intuit/futureofsmallbusiness/intuit_2020_report.pdf

Jay, R (2017) Top 30 companies hiring freelancers, 01/10 [Online] https://www.flexjobs.com/blog/post/top-30-companies-hiring-freelancers

Milbourn, T (2015) In the future, employees won't exist, 14/6 [Online] https://techcrunch.com/2015/06/13/in-the-future-employees-wont-exist/ [Last accessed 4.5.18]

PWC (2014) *The Future of Work: A journey to 2022* [Online] http://pwc.blogs.com/files/future-of-work-report-1.pdf

Strutz, M (2016) Freelancers and technology are leading the workforce revolution, 10/11 [Online] www.forbes.com/sites/berlinschoolofcreativeleadership/2016/11/10/free-lancers-and-technology-are-leading-the-workforce-revolution/#736f5c585d21

Technology Vision (2016) *Liquid Workforce: Building the workforce for today's digital demands* [Online] www.accenture.com/fr-fr/_acnmedia/PDF-2/Accenture-Liquid-Workforce-Technology-Vision-2016-france.pdf

Index

CPSIA information can be obtained
at www.ICGtesting.com
Printed in the USA
BVHW06s1345171018
530422BV00027B/567/P